THE KNIGHTS TEMPLAR

THE
KNIGHTS TEMPLAR

THEIR HISTORY AND MYTHS REVEALED

ALAN BUTLER

SHELTER HARBOR PRESS

NEW YORK

Text © 2011 by Alan Butler

Design and layout © 2014 by Alexian Limited

This 2014 edition published by Shelter Harbor
Press by arrangement with Alexian Limited

Picture credits
All images included in this volume are in the
public domain, with the exception of the
following, for whom the publishers gratefully
acknowledge permission:
Amaianos (pp.10–11)
Anjamation (p.85)
Bridgeman Art Library (p.41, p.133)
Simon Brighton (p.81, p.169)
Corbis (p.67, p.81, p.175)
Mary Evans Picture Library (p.53)
Theodor Scott (p.142 bottom)

The maps are by Lorraine Harrison

Cataloging-in-Publication Data has been
applied for and may be obtained from the
Library of Congress.

Shelter Harbor Press
603 W. 115th Street
Suite 163
New York, NY 10025

ISBN: 978-1-62795-010-7

Printed and bound in Thailand

10 9 8 7 6 5 4 3 2 1

Contents

Foreword   6

1   A clash of cultures   10

2   The rise of Champagne   26

3   A journey to Jerusalem   38

4   A new order of white monks   50

5   An official order of fighting knights   64

6   Monks at home and at war   78

7   Bankers, builders and tax collectors   94

8   Triumph and disaster   112

9   Dark days   130

10 Templar mysteries   144

    Epilogue   172

    Glossary   182

    Bibliography   189

    Index   191

Foreword

At dawn on Friday 13 October 1307, soldiers loyal to King Philip IV of France burst into churches, farms and preceptories throughout the entire kingdom. Their aim was to apprehend and imprison as many members of a particular religious community as they could – and with the utmost force if necessary. But the monks who would be taken off in chains to face torture and death were no ordinary holy brothers – they were the Knights Templar.

For two centuries the Knights Templar had represented the most successful and ultimately the richest monastic institution the world had ever seen. The original intention of the Order had been to supply armed knights to assist in Christianity's struggle against the encroaching armies of Islam. In and around Jerusalem, Templar knights fought with courage and tenacity, but the Knights Templar were to become much more than a group of holy soldiers.

The "Poor Knights of Christ and the Temple of Solomon" became officially recognized by the Catholic Church as a monastic institution in 1128. From the outset they recognized no other authority than that of the pope and became a virtual private army, dedicated to

▲ Templar Knights at Carcasonne, a modern interpretation by Corinne Heline.

◀ "The Old City" is a 0.9 square kilometer walled area within the modern city of East Jerusalem.

safeguarding Jerusalem and the Near East.

From their inception in the twelfth century, the Knights Templar spread across Europe and beyond with startling speed. Becoming massively popular, they received gifts of land and money, which they used wisely to gain more property and wealth elsewhere. The Templars created a large navy of fighting and cargo ships; they became the world's first true bankers, travel agents and were at the leading edge of the technology of their day. Templars brought about new building techniques, creating some of the most amazing castles and churches the medieval world would see.

Members of the Knights Templar were fully fledged monks, brothers of the equally successful Cistercian Order, from which they had sprung. In the fullness of time the Order of the Temple was a positive phenomenon and quite quickly Templar preceptories were to be found in every part of Europe and the Near East. Templar ships could be seen in the Baltic, the Black Sea, across the Mediterranean and around the coasts of Western Europe. The Order also built and guarded roads and important trade routes over huge distances.

So rich and influential did the Knights Templar become that they eventually held the fortunes of kings and kingdoms in their hands. They openly arbitrated between warring kings and barons, and could even put pressure on bishops and popes, who relied on the Knights' business acumen and military might.

From a nucleus of only nine members, who had been garrisoned over the ruins of the legendary Temple of Solomon in Jerusalem, the Knights Templar grew to an institution that supported thousands of individuals – all dedicated to expanding the frontiers and business potential of the Order.

The Knights Templar was a tremendously successful organization. So what caused it to become suddenly public enemy number one, not only to kings but also to the Pope, the head of the very Church for which the Templars had fought so tenaciously and so bravely? What was so special about this religious order and what, if anything, had its first brothers discovered beneath the Temple Mound in the sacred city of Jerusalem? Were the Templars really guilty of the most profound heresy of which they were accused in 1307? What actually happened to the majority of the Templar knights and their vast treasures, which slipped right through the fingers of King Philip IV in 1307?

The importance of the Knights Templar cannot be underestimated, even today. Much of the way the Western world functions, especially in a financial sense, is thanks to models put in place by Templarism, which was a tremendously modern institution in its time. Templarism broke the bonds of feudalism and allowed money and goods to flow across national boundaries in a way it had not done since the heyday of Rome. It also indirectly decreased the power of both Church and St.ate, offering merchants new, safe and sometimes very distant markets, where luxury goods could be exchanged for traditional produce such as wool.

▲ The Knights Templars were the elite fighting force of their day, highly trained, well-equipped and highly motivated.

The tale of the Knights Templar is also the story of the extraordinary region of Champagne in France, where forward thinking and shrewd planning had allowed the Templars to be created. Safe in their headquarters in Troyes, capital of Champagne, the Templars survived for almost two centuries. But when the end came and the world turned against the Templars, was their whole empire consigned to the annals of dusty history books? Many researchers and writers do not believe this was the case. And in numerous different forms, the influence of the most extraordinary monastic order ever created can still be experienced seven centuries on.

Some researchers see a direct link between the Knights Templar and the later but equally significant institution of Freemasonry. It has been suggested that Templarism lay at the heart of Rosicrucianism and that they may have been planning to reconcile Judaism, Islam and Christianity into one cohesive world religion.

Somewhere between myth and fact lies the truth of the Knights Templar. With their white tunics bearing the famous red cross, those fearless warriors have become an icon of chivalry to many, but to others they still represent the spawn of the Devil. One fact is not in doubt: without the influence of the Knights Templar, the world in which we live today would most certainly have been very different.

▼ Ponferrada, in the province of León, Spain, is noted for its Castillo de los Templarios or Templar Castle. In 1178 Ferdinand II of León gave the Templars the right to use the city to protect pilgrims on their way to the shrine of St. James in Santiago de Compostela, and the castle was built to mark this honor.

1

A clash of cultures

THE RISE OF ISLAM AND THE FIRST CRUSADE

At the end of the eleventh century, Christianity was facing its greatest threat since the days of the anti-Christian Roman Emperors. The religion of Islam was rapidly expanding from its point of origin in the Middle East and was now threatening the East and South of Europe. Huge armies of Muslim soldiers were poised to overthrow Eastern Christianity, based in Constantinople, and the very future of the faith was under threat.

Islam had come into being in the Middle East in the seventh century. It soon gained popularity and power, and began to spread under the Abbasid Caliphate north, east and west, engulfing Egypt and extending up to the borders of the Byzantine Empire. Muslims from the North African coast attacked and conquered southern Spain, then began to push north, threatening the soft underbelly of Christian Western Europe.

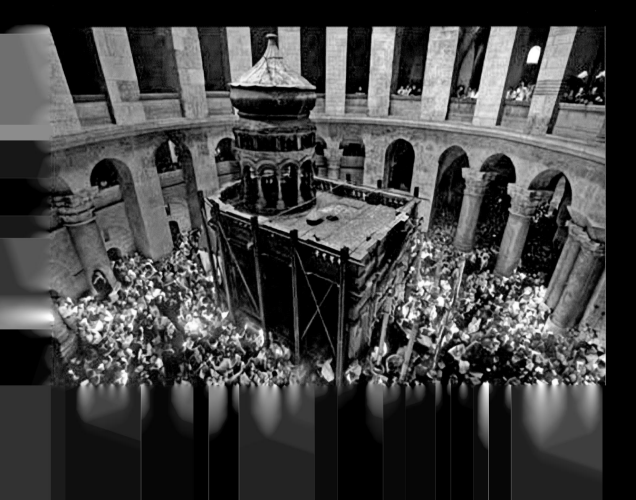

A modern depiction of what a "chivalrous crusader" Templar knight would have looked like.

Christian pilgrims hold candles at the Church of the Holy Sepulcher in Jerusalem, traditionally believed to be the site of the crucifixion of Jesus Christ, during the ceremony of the Holy Fire. The ceremony dates back to the twelfth century.

It was under these circumstances that crusading came into being. For some decades prior to the eleventh century the Near East, including the ancient city of Jerusalem, was in the hands of Muslim rulers. Jerusalem was a sacred city to Jews, Christians and Muslims alike, but though Christians were still allowed to visit the Holy Land on pilgrimage, it was becoming more difficult and dangerous to do so. Many Christians believed that in order to protect the faith in the East and to save Jerusalem from what they saw as its imprisonment, it would be necessary to raise a huge army that could defeat the Muslims once and for all.

To arrange such a military expedition from Europe would be a logistical nightmare. Most states at the time were feudal and quite insular. Powerful barons fought each other and kingdoms clashed regularly. Few kings were powerful enough to raise armies that would need to travel thousands of kilometers or miles to reach the battlefield. However, the arrival on the scene of a powerful pope, named Urban II, who was elected in 1088, gave new impetus to Christians fighting side by side in order to protect their faith. The Christian Church had been split into two basic units – Eastern and

Western Christianity – and the two Churches had been squabbling for several centuries. Pope Urban II wanted to reunite the faith in its common cause against the spread of Islam.

It was these circumstances that paved the way for the conception of the "chivalrous knight," a fearless warrior dedicated to protecting the weak and safeguarding Christianity. Several groups of holy soldiers, some of whom were priests, came into existence. These included the Knights Hospitaller, an order that had first arisen as early as around 1023, but the Poor Knights of Christ and the Temple of Solomon, better known today as the Knights Templar, was the most successful of these military orders.

◀ The Templars were both monks and soldiers, making them some of the earliest "warrior monks" in the Western world. Members of the Order played a key part in many battles of the Crusades.

A call to arms

In November of 1095 a great ecclesiastical gathering took place in Clermont, France. The Council of Clermont had been called by Pope Urban II and he arrived in France determined to solve a number of the Church's problems at a stroke. In particular he wanted to curb the spread of Islam, to make a new effort to bring the Christian West and East together, and to promote common aims within Western Christian states that were often fighting each other. The West was filled with anti-Islamic sentiment and people listened avidly to terrible stories of Christians on pilgrimage in the Holy Land being assaulted and even murdered.

▼ Pope Urban II blessing the First Crusade.

At the end of the Council of Clermont, Urban II delivered what was to become a famous speech in which he talked of the difficulties being encountered by fellow believers in the East and especially in Constantinople. The Pope urged all able-bodied knights to put their arms to the service of the Church and to join a powerful army that could overthrow the Saracens – the name by which Christians referred to Muslims at the time. In reality the Pope already had his mind set on conquering the Holy Land, and Jerusalem in particular. The Pope was the head of the Roman or Western Church and had little authority in the East. The possession of the city held holiest by Christianity would reinforce the powerbase of the Vatican and also demonstrate a strong Western presence in the Holy Land.

Urban's call to arms proved to be extremely popular, but it did not take place in isolation. Around the same time Christianity in Western Europe was receiving a boost from those who saw the faith as having become lax and corrupt. New and quite revolutionary forms of monasticism were coming into being, with new churches and abbeys springing up everywhere. The old, mostly Benedictine order of monasticism had become slipshod, but from the eleventh century on reorganized monasticism spawned daughter houses from great abbeys such as Cluny in northern France, and created pockets of austere monasticism that were modeled on the ways of the desert fathers of Christianity's early days. These truly poor and extremely pious monks became popular with the secular masses.

▲ Pope Urban II at the Council of Clermont, given a late Gothic setting in this illumination from the *Livre des Passages d'Outre-mer*, of ca.1490.

▶ Detail of medieval crusading knights from the stained glass window at *Sainte Chapelle*, "The Holy Chapel," a gothic chapel on the Île de la Cité in the heart of Paris.

▲ Cluny Abbey, a Benedictine monastery in Cluny, Saône-et-Loire, France. It was built in the Romanesque style, with three churches built in succession from the 10th to the early 12th centuries. Cluny was founded by William I, Duke of Aquitaine in 910.

Islam on the move

At the beginning of the sixth century the Arabian Peninsula had been a place of fragmented states and beliefs. Many Arabs were nomadic traders or herders owing tribal allegiance and worshipping a variety of different gods and goddesses. The arrival of the prophet Muhammad, born in Mecca in 570 AD, brought cohesion and would eventually lead to the people of Arabia and far beyond committing to a single religious and political vision.

Muhammad believed himself to be the last and most important prophet of God. After a somewhat shaky start, he began to gain converts, especially in the city of Medina. From this base the forces of Islam began to spread out and to bring the new religion to peoples outside of Arabia. Exploiting constant battles between the Byzantine and Persian Empires, the Caliphs, who controlled Islam after the death of Muhammad in 632, made rapid progress. By 646 AD, Arab armies had taken control of Syria, which was soon followed by Iraq and then the greater part of Egypt by 640.

Islam continued to spread its influence into Africa and also out into the Mediterranean. Much of Europe was split into a multitude of small, feudal states, which had been created with the fall of the Roman Empire during the fifth century. Christianity in the far West had been temporarily replaced by barbarism as Germanic tribes had flooded down into France and across into Britain. It took time for kingdoms such as that of the Franks in France to form and to be Christianized and even Christian

▼ Al-Masjid al-Nabawi (the Mosque of the Prophet) in Medina, Saudi Arabia, is the site of Muhammad's tomb.

fighting Christian was a common theme across three centuries in Europe. By 711 AD there was a most horrifying vision for European Christians in the form of Islamic armies attacking southern Spain. By the end of the eleventh century, Islam had also made great inroads into the Byzantine Empire (the name by which the Eastern Roman Empire came to be known), which would have a tremendous impact not only on religion but also on established Christian trade routes to the Far East. It was the attack of the Seljuk Turks and the Byzantine army's disaster at Muslim hands in 1071 that caused the Byzantine Emperor, Alexius Comnenus, to call upon Western Europe and the Pope for armed assistance.

▲ Mecca is a city in the Makkah province of Saudi Arabia. Islamic tradition attributes the beginning of Mecca to Ishmael"s descendants. The modern day city is the capital of Saudi Arabia's Makkah Province, in the historic Hejaz region. It is regarded as the holiest city in Islam.

The sons of Lords

At the same time as Byzantium came under threat, Christianity in the West had another major problem that had originated within its own borders. The feudal kingdoms that had gradually developed after the fall of the Roman Empire had come to be ruled by monarchs who relied greatly on powerful landed families to control their domains and people their armies. These dynasties of barons and lords were unquestioned rulers in their own lands and constantly battled with one another for greater holdings and influence.

▼ Mounted knights with shields as depicted in the Bayeux tapestry.

This was also the age of the mounted knight – the tank of his day, who could spread death and destruction on a huge scale against lightly armed infantry. Wealth gave way to luxurious living, the population grew and the baronial families became larger. Now lords had many sons, all of whom were brought up from infancy to be fearless warriors. This created a problem: what could all these heavily armed young men do with their time? The answer seemed to be that they constantly found newer and better ways to wage war against each other.

The ordinary peasants and also the Church were frequently caught in the middle of these squabbles. Religious institutions were openly attacked and Church property was desecrated. The peasantry called upon their priests and bishops to protect them, and the bishops turned to the pope. By the reign of Urban II, the situation was getting completely out of hand and the Pope realized that useful employment for the sons of feudal lords abroad would prevent the squabbling at home. This would safeguard ordinary Christians and leave Church property and personnel unmolested.

And so the age of chivalry dawned, with the concept of the courageous and powerful knight taking up the cross and using his fighting acumen for the good of the Church and on behalf of the weak.

At the time armies began to assemble in order to mount the First Crusade, Muslim states in the Holy Land, in Egypt and in Syria had become quite fragmented. In the early days of the faith, Islamic armies had willingly fought together, but with the passing of time, dynastic and political interests across such a vast area gained more importance than

▲ In 1095 Pope Urban II launched the First Crusade. Christian knights, men-at-arms and peasants, the largest army the world had seen in centuries, marched across Europe to wage a "Holy War." The spearhead of the Crusade was mostly poor men, women and children without property or political obligations who could mobilise faster than the mighty European warring classes. Led by charismatic religious leaders and a few enterprizing Frankish and German Knights, this first group was dubbed "The People's Crusade."

▲ The Siege of Jerusalem as depicted in a medieval manuscript. The First Crusade was a military expedition by European Christians to regain the Holy Lands taken by the Muslim conquest of the Levant, finally resolving in the capture of Jerusalem in 1099.

religion. This led to a greater initial success on the part of the crusaders. Pope Urban II had suggested that the crusade should commence on 15 August 1096, but a sizeable proportion of peasants and some less important nobles set off earlier, in April of the same year, under the leadership of a charismatic preacher known as Peter the Hermit. This earlier foray east proved to be a military disaster, but it did firm up resolve in Western Europe for the more organized crusade that was to follow.

Crusader knights came from many parts of Western Europe, but the region of France probably contributed the most. The number of soldiers who began the long journey east may well have numbered as many as 30,000–35,000, of whom around 5,000 were armed knights.

▶ Peter the Hermit leading the Crusades, 1311. From *Abreviamen de las Estorias*, early 14th century.

The journey was fraught with difficulties, not least the degree of infighting that took place between the various factions of crusaders. However, significant victories against the Turks, particularly the capture of Konya, capital of the Seljuk Turks, in 1097 led to an uneasy truce between traditional enemies among the Christian armies and somehow kept the project going. By 1099 a significant amount of territory had been captured and the crusading armies stood before the city walls of Jerusalem.

It was on 15 July 1099 that a much depleted but nevertheless determined crusader army finally broke down the defenses of Jerusalem and stormed into the city. Terrible carnage followed as both Muslims and Jews were indiscriminately put to the sword. People back in Europe and the Pope especially were elated in the knowledge that the holiest city of all was now in Christian hands.

▲ The conquering of Jerusalem during the First Crusade. For 39 days Crusaders besieged the Holy City, until it finally fell on 15 July 1099 and they replaced the crescent with the cross on the Dome of the Rock.

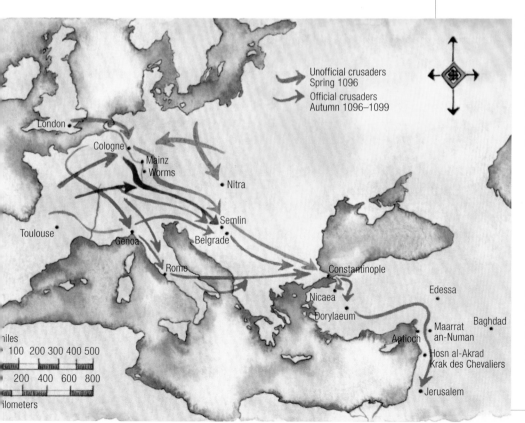

Unofficial crusaders
Spring 1096
Official crusaders
Autumn 1096–1099

London
Cologne
Mainz
Worms
Nitra
Toulouse
Genoa
Semlin
Belgrade
Rome
Constantinople
Nicaea
Edessa
Dorylaeum
Baghdad
Maarrat an-Numan
Antioch
Hosn al-Akrad
Krak des Chevaliers
Jerusalem

miles
100 200 300 400 500

200 400 600 800
kilometers

◄ Map showing the routes of the unofficial and official crusaders during the First Crusade of 1096–1099.

▲ Baldwin of Boulogne, one of the leaders of the First Crusade, entering Edessa in February 1098. A painting by J. Robert-Fleury (1797–1890).

Many saw this as starting the era of the "New Jerusalem" that was mentioned, particularly in the book of Revelation, in the Bible.

The first difficulty encountered once Jerusalem and large areas of the Near East had been captured lay in establishing how to control them. At first, rule of much of the captured area fell to a French noble by the name of Godfrey de Bouillon. Godfrey was reluctant to be declared king of Jerusalem. Instead, he took the title of "Defender of the Holy Sepulcher," which was the most revered Christian church in the city. Unfortunately, Godfrey lived for only a short time after the capture of Jerusalem, dying in 1100.

After Godfrey's death, rule of Jerusalem and most of the crusader states passed to his brother, Baldwin of Boulogne (who therefore became Baldwin I). Somewhat reluctantly he accepted the title of King of Jerusalem, but though hedged around by problems and always short of fighting men, he proved an able ruler.

When Baldwin I died in 1118, he was replaced on the throne of Jerusalem by a cousin, Baldwin of Rethel. Almost as soon as Baldwin II came to power, his kingdom was invaded by Muslims from both Syria and Egypt. One of his basic problems lay in the fact that many of the

original crusader knights had returned to their own lands almost as soon as Jerusalem had been captured. The Western European knights still there were far from their homes, and lines of communication and supply were stretched to breaking point. If the Near East were to remain in the hands of the European Christians, a large, capable and well-provisioned standing army would be required. With renewed spiritual energy taking the West by storm, part of this void was filled by newly formed military orders, such as the fighting monks of the Knights Templar. However, the story of the Templars is also the story of the rise of one particular region of France, which would prove to be one of the greatest success stories feudal Europe would ever know.

▲ Baldwin II ceding the Temple of Solomon to Hugues de Payns and Gaudefroy de Saint-Homer. Hughes de Payns (Hughes de Pagan/ Hugh of Payens/Hugh Pagan) (ca.1070–1136), a French knight from the Champagne region, was the co-founder and first Grand Master of the Knights Templar.

2

The rise of Champagne

THE SUCCESS OF THIS BUSY INDUSTRIAL REGION WAS PRIMARILY DUE
TO ITS FAMOUS FAIRS, AND THE WEALTH GAINED BY COMMERCE WAS
TRANSMUTED INTO THE BEAUTY AND GLORY OF ITS BUILDINGS

No region of western Europe failed to send its most famous and courageous knights to fight in the First Crusade, though France may well have contributed more soldiers than any other single area. Around this time the actual kingdom of France was quite small. It was bounded in the north by Flanders (modern Netherlands and Belgium), in the west by Normandy and to the south by Burgundy. The French domains were centerd mainly around Paris. After the withdrawal of the Roman forces in the fifth and sixth centuries, France had eventually become united under a people known as the Franks, who had arrived from Germany and conquered virtually all of what had once been Gaul. Later incursions, particularly by the Vikings, and a break-up of Frankish Gaul into smaller units, meant that by the tenth century the kings of France were only nominal rulers of the whole area.

The main reason for the state of affairs that predominated as the eleventh century approached was that, with time, the Frankish tradition of dividing lands among surviving sons had meant that the greater area had become split into smaller units. Some of these were totally independent but others, such as Champagne, owed allegiance to the French crown at the time. The same was also true, in some periods at least, of Burgundy and Flanders. However, as fortunes changed and dynastic holdings were split and then consolidated, often by marriage, the situation altered dramatically across time.

◄ Setting out on a crusade. Not only Princes and knights, but also peasants and servants rose en masse to go against the infidels. The wealthy and poor, men and women, old men and youths, all sold everything to make the expedition of God.

As the end of the eleventh century approached, the rulers of Champagne owed fealty to France. This meant they would support the King of France in time of war and since the kings of France also held lands in Champagne, the Crown also gained financially from the situation. Despite its fealty to France, the region of Champagne, which was centered around the ancient city of Troyes, to the south and east of the French domains, gradually became fiercely independent. The main reason for this growing independence lay in the fact that Champagne was ruled by a powerful aristocracy headed by a "Count." The aristocracy could in turn call on the support of their own vassals and field a formidable army if necessary. In an age when "might was right," this state of affairs meant that the successive counts of Champagne could hold their own against the French Crown.

▶ Champagne gained importance during the Middle Ages as a center of European trade. The medieval counts of Champagne encouraged commerce and protected the traveling merchants. They created the then famous, Fairs of Champagne.

Part of Champagne's importance lay in its strategic position. It was located at an important crossroads along which merchants brought luxury goods, some of which came from as far away as both the Near and the Middle East. It was also significant with regard to north–south trade within France and Western Europe as a whole. The counts of Champagne sought to exploit this fact from a very early date and established merchant markets, known as the "Champagne Fairs." To these gatherings came merchants from all corners of the known world.

Champagne also became an important spiritual and cultural center, where Christians and Jews cooperated and where the rule of law allowed a peaceful and settled existence. Most important of all, Champagne became extremely rich. It attracted intellectuals and produced spiritual leaders, whose presence would eventually change the Roman Catholic Church significantly. The most influential of these were Pope Urban II (Pope from 1088 to 1099) who had been born in Champagne and who showed a preference for the region as a result, and Bernard of Clairvaux (1090–1153), a Cistercian abbot who, although never a pope himself, probably had even more power than one and was certainly a "pope maker." Urban II was responsible for commencing the Crusades in order to wrest the Near East from Islam, and Bernard of Clairvaux helped to shift the balance of power within the Catholic Church away from Rome itself. It was within this extraordinary region of France that the Knights Templar came into being.

At the crossroads

Co-operation and trade were not the hallmarks of a generally feudal Western Europe at the dawn of the crusading age. As a political system, feudalism relied on lesser and greater lords, who came together willingly to support the king of a particular region. Battles between regions were common and boundaries changed frequently. None of this particularly fostered cross-border trade.

The population of Europe was growing rapidly. Food supplies and raw materials of all kinds were required in regions that could not provide for all their own needs. At the same time, many of the local lords who had traveled to the East on crusade had become familiar with the silks, spices and other commodities that were brought by caravans, sometimes all the way from China, and which ultimately found their way into the markets of the Middle and Near East. With the Near East in the hands of the Western powers, merchandise arriving in the area could be more readily traded into Western Europe. Safe environments were required in which merchants from East and West could come together in order to exchange their commodities to meet their needs.

Nowhere was better suited geographically than Champagne to supply what the merchants required. Champagne stood astride important roads that led northwards to Flanders and eventually up to the Baltic. Firs from the north, wool from Britain and finished woolen cloth from Flanders were

▼ The Cloth Hall of Ypres was one of the largest commercial buildings of the Middle Ages. It served as the main market and warehouse for the Flemish city's prosperous cloth industry. Built mainly in the thirteenth century and completed in 1304, it was almost completely destroyed under artillery fire in the First World War.

taken to this region at a very early date. There these items met the more exotic products that were being shipped across the Mediterranean to southern France, and so it was only natural that the region gathered importance as a center of international trade.

Impromptu gatherings of merchants in Troyes had taken place for centuries, as they did everywhere. They had originally served the people of the locality, but not long after the First Crusade the counts of Champagne began to turn their attention to formalizing the merchant gatherings. They did so to attract traders from much further away and to create trade links that would eventually become vital to the development of Europe.

▼ Vineyards in Verzena, the Montagne de Reims subregion of Champagne. The region's reputation for wine production dates back to the Middle Ages.

The Champagne Fairs

The word "fair" might give the impression of enjoyable social gatherings, but the medieval version was dramatically different. There were six fairs each year in Champagne. Two took place in Troyes, two in Provins, one in Bar-sur-Aube and one in Lagny. They were spaced throughout the year and each gathering lasted for several weeks. All four towns eventually built large warehouses, where the goods of the merchants attending the fairs could be stored and well guarded. Accommodation and good policing of the fairs was also arranged, so that no merchant needed to fear for the security of his gold.

All manner of goods were traded at the Champagne Fairs, but the emphasis was definitely on woolen cloth and Champagne eventually became a great "clearing house." Raw wool from north-west Europe, and especially Britain, was shipped to Flanders, where it was sorted, spun and woven into cloth. The cloth was then shipped to Champagne, where it was traded for more exotic goods, mostly by Italians. The cloth was then sent off to Italy where it was dyed and finished to a high standard. Some of this richly finished cloth also found its way back to the Champagne Fairs at subsequent gatherings.

Along with woolen cloth, the merchants traded linen, firs, drugs and medicines, and luxury goods from the Near and Far East. Traders would spend the bulk of the fairs haggling over prices and delivery, and towards the end of each fair a reckoning would be made. At first, merchants were expected to meet their commitments promptly in cash or to exchange goods, but with the fullness of time the Champagne

▼ Carding, dying and spinning wool, from a fourteenth century French illumination.

▲ Provins was famous in the twelfth and thirteenth centuries for its huge trading fairs, or foires, after the Counts of Champagne introduced a passport of safe passage across their territory for merchants.

Fairs became a center of embryonic credit transactions of the sort that would become the lifeblood of the Knights Templar. In fact the credit transactions started quite early at the Champagne Fairs, certainly by the middle of the twelfth century. They were made possible because of the security of the region and also because the rules and regulations to which all merchants agreed meant a merchant's word truly was his bond. If anyone participating defaulted on an agreement to pay for goods at a specified time, he would be banned from attending the Champagne Fairs in future. The Knights Templar simply took a principle that worked extremely well in the local context of Champagne, and gradually expanded it across a much greater geographical area.

In reality, all the mechanisms of trade eventually required by the Knights Templar were already in place before the Order even came into existence. Most of these had been created over the merchants' tables at the Champagne Fairs – the very region that gave birth to the Templars.

No commodity at the Champagne Fairs was more important than wool, for as the population of Europe began to grow, wool became a most important commodity. Sheep had been raised in Western Europe since the late St.one Age, but the first domestic sheep had been kept predominantly for milk and meat. Wool had been used for clothing, but it took selective breeding across a long period before something like the wool-bearing sheep we know today were created.

◀ "Sheep Shearing" by Jean, Duc de Berry, *Books of Hours* (ca.1410). Shears in the middle ages were mainly used to cut the fleece from sheep.

▼ The Master of the Knights Templar's great seal was double-sided and showed the picture of The Dome of the Rock on one side and the Order's symbol of two knights on one horse on the other side. There was also a smaller, single-sided seal, which showed the Dome of the Rock (or the circular dome of the Holy Sepulcher). Every Grand Master seal shares distinctive characteristics. In order to avoid misuse, special measures were taken regarding the seals. They were kept in a locked compartment which required three keys to open. The Grand Master himself kept one of these keys, and two of his high officials held the others. The forgery of the seals was a very difficult process because each seal was unique and hand made.

Sheep could live on very marginal land and were adapted to a variety of conditions and temperatures. This made them an ideal species for the fringes of Western Europe – for example, the marshy lands of Flanders and the harsh uplands of Britain. They also needed little attention in order to flourish.

Both the Knights Templar and the monastic order of the Cistercians from which they sprang would become experts in the breeding and raising of sheep, and it would be fair to say that a high proportion of the wealth of both institutions came directly from sheep. It is therefore not at all

▲ During the First Crusade there was no official leader but two or three gradually emerged and the greatest of these was Godfrey de Bouillon who led the knights from Lorraine, Belgium and other "Low Countries" area.

▶ Monastery of Vimbodí i Poblet. This Cistercian monastery, founded in 1151 Cistercian monks from France, is located in the comarca of Conca de Barberà, in Catalonia, Spain. It was the first of three sister monasteries, known as the Cistercian triangle, that helped consolidate power in Catalonia in the twelfth century (the other two are Vallbona de les Monges and Santes Creus). This monastery was abandoned in 1835 and was restored during the 1940s.

surprizing that the most famous symbol of the Knights Templar, the "Agnus Dei" ("Lamb of God"), is still to be seen everywhere the order flourished. The Agnus Dei is far from simply a religious symbol denoting Jesus Christ. Rather it demonstrates the humble creature upon which so much wealth and power originally depended.

The counts and aristocrats of Champagne had been among the first to volunteer to fight in the First Crusade. They had been in the entourage of Godfrey de Bouillon, whose detachment broke the siege of the city in 1099. The leading families of Champagne were tied by blood to those, such as Godfrey, who would become the earliest Christian kings of the holy city, and history shows that the potential of the Christian Near East was not lost on them.

It is surely no coincidence that the moment the Holy Land and its critical trade routes were secured, the Count of Champagne immediately began

to pour money into improving and enlarging the Champagne Fairs. But this is far from the only change that was taking place in Champagne at this most pivotal period. Christian monasticism was undergoing what would turn out to be its most significant revolution. This was a response to the perceived laxity of the Benedictine order, which had first been created in the sixth century. With the passing of time many Benedictine abbeys had become colossally rich. Abbots controlled vast areas of land and the original "spirituality" and poverty of the order had been seriously eroded. A natural zeal that accompanied the fight against Islam and the crusades themselves helped to inspire many monks to seek a more austere life, one that they perceived to be closer to the original Benedictine ideal. New orders of monks were developing as a result. Some were very specialized, such as the Order of Tironensians, who would become famed for their acumen in building.

However, the most important of the new monastic adventures would be that of the Cistercians, from which the Order of the Templars would soon emerge. As with the Tironensians, the Cistercian order owed its creation and its early success to the aristocratic families of Champagne. Although the first of the Cistercian monasteries was located in northern Burgundy, the land upon which it stood was given by the counts of Champagne. What was more, the real leading light of early Cistercianism, Bernard of Clairvaux, was an aristocrat who was related to the Champagne counts and who ruled his own abbey at Clairvaux, just a few kilometers (or a couple of miles) from Troyes.

▼ St. Bernard of Clairvaux (1091–1153), one of the first Cistercian monks, was third medieval father and last father of the Church in chronological order. He was canonized in 1174 by Pope Alexander III and Pope Pius VII declared him a Doctor of the Church in 1830.

3

A journey to Jerusalem

NINE KNIGHTS AND SECRETS UNDER THE TEMPLE MOUNT

The story of the origins of the Knights Templar was only related decades after the event. It comes from the pen of a man by the name of Guillaume de Tyr (ca.1130–1186), a chronicler and archbishop of Tyre. In his account, Guillaume tells of nine knights, mostly aristocrats and led by a kinsman of the Count of Champagne, who suddenly and quite mysteriously banded together for an extraordinary mission. If the historical accounts are to be believed, these nine men, all penniless and absolutely dependent on the charity of the King of Jerusalem, set off to the Holy Land in 1118 with only one intention – to offer support and protection to pilgrims traveling along the dusty and dangerous roads between the coast of the Mediterranean and Jerusalem.

Is it really very likely that only nine men, no matter how devout and committed, could ever have represented anything like the police force historians declared them to be? What is more, there is not the slightest tangible evidence that the embryonic Templar Order ever undertook such a role. The only information at our disposal indicates that the knights in question rarely if ever left the confines of Jerusalem. Had they been active in their intended role as protectors of pilgrims, their presence would have been mentioned in sources from the period but in fact,

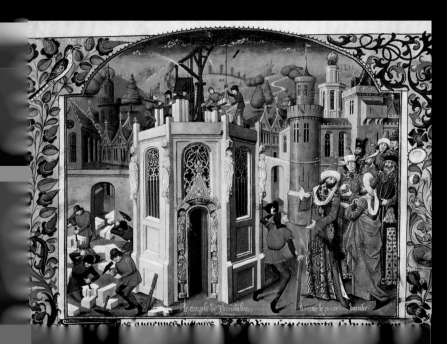

◀ Sultan Omar rebuilds the Temple in Jerusalem. From Guillaume de Tyr, "Histoire de la Conquete de Jerusalem," Ms.fr 2629, folio 17. French fifteenth-century illuminated manuscript. Bibliotheque Nat.,Coll. des Manuscrits, Paris, France.

apart from the work of Guillaume de Tyr, we hear nothing of the first Templar knights. As to any information from the Order itself, all documentation eventually passed to the Knights of St. John (Knights Hospitaller), but was lost when their headquarters in Cyprus were destroyed by the Turks in 1571.

What we do know, thanks to Guillaume de Tyr, is that the first Templar knights traveled to Jerusalem in 1118, but as far as any documentation is concerned, they disappeared entirely from the historical record for over a decade. During this period they sought no recruits and in fact the only newcomer to swell their ranks was the Count of Champagne himself, Hughes I, who abdicated his position in 1124 and apparently became as impoverished and dependent on the charity of others as his companion knights. What is more, Hughes threw himself under the authority of Hugues de Payen, a man of lower rank.

It is not known exactly what the first Templar knights were doing for over a decade, but what seems most likely is that they were busily occupied in some endeavor that would ensure their meteoric rise when the circumstances and political atmosphere proved to be just right.

▷ Hugues de Payen (1070–1136) was the first grand master and founder of the Order of the Temple and one of the first nine knights. He served in the army of Godfrey of Bouillon during the First Crusade. The Order, founded in Jerusalem, later became the Temple, and its statutes were approved by the Council of Troyes in 1128. Payens led the Order for almost twenty years until his death.

A historical source

As we have seen, the main source of evidence (in fact practically the only source) relating to the origins of the Knights Templar comes from Guillaume de Tyr. He was born in Jerusalem in 1130, of French parents. Although not of noble blood, Guillaume was capable and astute. He chose a career as a churchman and diplomat, especially in the service of King Amalric I (Christian king of Jerusalem and successor to Baldwin III) and also Pope Alexander III. Eventually, in 1175 he became the Bishop of Tyre.

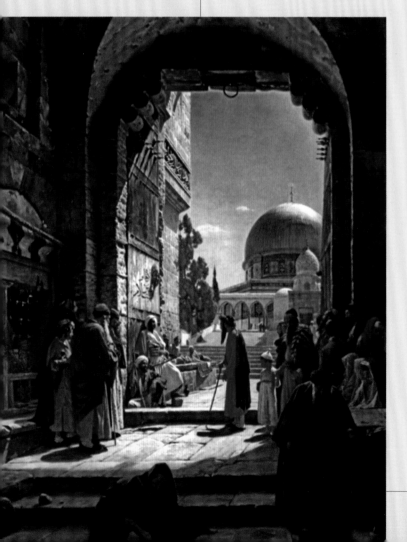

▼ "At the Entrance to the Temple Mount, Jerusalem," 1886. An oil painting by Gustave Bauernfeind (1848–1904).

Today Guillaume de Tyr is best known for the history of Christian Jerusalem that he began in around 1170. It is known as *A History of Deeds Done Beyond the Sea* and this account includes details relating to the first Templar knights. However, the events it describes took place nearly half a century earlier and it is not known whether Guillaume's account of the first Templars is accurate.

It is Guillaume who tells us that the nine knights came to Jerusalem in 1118 and that there they presented themselves to Baldwin II, who had come to the throne of Jerusalem in April of the same year. They appealed to his charity and asked for lodgings. Baldwin granted the knights the right to occupy part of the stables on the Temple Mount in Jerusalem, immediately above the ruins of the Jewish Temple that had once stood on the site and adjacent to his own palace.

The knights in question are listed as being: Hugues de Payen (their leader), André de Montbard, Geoffroi de St. Omer, Payen de Montdidier, Achambaud de St.-Amand, Geoffroi Bisol, Gondemare, Rosal and Godfroi. The very idea that these were truly penniless men of humble origins disappears immediately when some of their backgrounds are examined.

Hugues de Payen was a landed aristocrat and a kinsman of the counts of Champagne, while André de Montbard was another Champagne-born man from a distinctly elevated family. We do however know that André de Montbard had both Champagne and Burgundy connections, and that he was the brother of Bernard of Clairvaux's mother. Both Payen de Montdidier and Achambaud de St.-Amand were closely related to the ruling house of Flanders. Geoffroi de St. Omer was almost certainly the son of Hughes de St. Omer, who had been a high-ranking crusader knight who became Prince of Galilee and Lord of Tiberius immediately after the First Crusade in 1101. We know little or nothing of the other men mentioned, but if there had been a *Who's Who* of Europe at this time at least half of the original Templar knights would certainly have warranted significant entries.

What adds to the mystery of the story is that we know that the original nine knights were joined in Jerusalem in 1124 by Count Hughes of Champagne. Hughes had voluntarily given up all his powers and possessions in Champagne and had passed the title of count on to his nephew. This led to a paradoxical twist that is almost incredible for the rank-obsessed period. The leader of the embryonic Templar movement was Hugues de Payen, who when in Champagne would have been a vassal of the Count. Now, in a virtually unparalleled reversal, Count Hughes became subservient to Hugues de Payen.

▲ William of Tyre, *A History of Deeds Done Beyond the Sea*, with a sequel leading up to 1275 (ca.1280). William of Tyre wrote this chronicle in Latin retracing the history of the Latin kingdom of Jerusalem up to 1184. An anonymous sequel concerning the years 1185–1194 was then written in England.

▲ The ancient city of Jerusalem with Solomon's Temple, ca.1871. Solomon's Temple, also known as the First Temple, was sited on Temple Mount (also known as Mount Zion), before its destruction by Nebuchadnezzar II after the Siege of Jerusalem of 587 BCE. According to the Hebrew Bible, the temple was constructed under Solomon, king of the Israelites. This would date its construction to the tenth century BCE. During the kingdom of Judah, the temple was dedicated to Yahweh, the God of Israel and housed the Ark of the Covenant. Only limited archaeological surveys of the Temple Mount have been conducted and there is no archaeological reconstruction of the temple as it stood at the time of its destruction by Nebuchadnezzar.

The location occupied by the original Templar knights in Jerusalem was one of the most famous and exalted places on Earth. Jerusalem was tremendously important to Christianity, since it figured constantly in the Old Testament of the Bible and was also the place of Jesus' trial, execution and resurrection. So important was the place to all Christians that on maps of the period Jerusalem almost always stood at the very center and was even known as "the navel of the world." And in the most important city in the world the most significant building had once been the Temple of Solomon, originally created around 950 BC as the most revered site of the Hebrews.

Solomon's Temple had housed the Ark of the Covenant, a gold-covered wooden box within which was stored the stone tablets, with the Ten Commandments written on them, brought down by Moses after he had encountered God on Mount Sinai. The Ark was kept in a portion of the building known as the "Holy of Holies" and it contained the Ten Commandments.

▶ Transporting the Ark of the Covenant, gilded brass relief, Cathedral of Sainte-Marie, Auch, France.

Although destroyed and rebuilt on several occasions, the Temple on the Mount in Jerusalem had contained untold treasure apart from the Ark of the Covenant. Over the centuries, large amounts of gold and silver adornments would have been offered as gifts to the Temple.

A document found among the Dead Sea Scrolls close to the River Jordan in the 1940s, dating back to a time just prior to the final destruction of the Temple, lists gold and silver to be found in many hiding places under the Temple itself. It is also likely that treasure of another sort, in the form of documents spanning many centuries, was also safeguarded in the tunnels.

The Temple itself was finally destroyed by the Romans in 70 AD. Subsequent Islamic rulers of Jerusalem had also revered the hilltop and today it is the site of a large mosque. The original Templars are known to have lived in the stables adjacent to King Baldwin II's palace, which stood right over the ruins of the original Temple.

It seems self-evident that the original Templar knights' reason for being in Jerusalem was quite different from the one ascribed to them by Guillaume de Tyr. There is not a single historical reference to the first knights guarding the roads from the Mediterranean coast to Jerusalem, which was their supposed mission in the Holy Land. In any case, such an undertaking would have been out of the question for nine men, no matter how dedicated they may have been. Nor did Hugues de Payen make any attempt during this first mysterious decade to enlarge his force. Hughes, former Count of Champagne, was the only recruit during the period. Guillaume de Tyr is quite specific regarding the arrival of the first Templars in Jerusalem and their supposed intention, but mentions nothing of their subsequent activities. In effect they literally disappeared from the pages of history for over a decade.

▲ "Solomon Dedicates the Temple at Jerusalem," ca.1896-1902, by James Jacques Joseph Tissot (1836–1902) (Jewish Museum, New York).

◀ The Dead Sea Scrolls were discovered in eleven caves along the northwest shore of the Dead Sea between 1947 and 1956. Fragments of every book of the Hebrew canon (Old Testament) have been discovered except for the book of Esther. In fact, the scrolls are the oldest group of Old Testament manuscripts ever found.

▲ By 1952, the caves in which the Dead Sea Scrolls had been found were under intense excavation, and on 14 March that year, inside "Cave 3," a copper scroll was discovered. The metal was heavily corroded and could not be unrolled. At Oxford University the scroll was carefully sliced into twenty-three strips and transcribed. It revealed a list of sixty-four locations, written down in twelve columns. Each entry was a treasure site: there were indications where gold, silver and other precious objects, like jewellery, perfumes and oils, had been hidden. The Copper Scroll appeared to be a treasure map!

▶ Map showing the old city of Jerusalem during the Crusader period.

In search of treasure?

In the absence of hard evidence, we have only legends to point to the real mission of Hugues de Payen and his men during the critical eleven years they disappear from written accounts. There is a persistent rumor, which seems to have begun at a very early date, that the first Templars were extremely busy during the whole of the time they inhabited the Temple Mount. It has been suggested for centuries that they were tunneling into the maze of corridors and shafts that marked the site of the original Temple.

If this was the case, what was it that Hugues de Payen and his men were seeking? There are many suggestions and these include the Ark of the Covenant. Many modern researchers pour scorn on such a suggestion, not least because the Ark seems to have disappeared from the annals of history at a very early date and even before the destruction of the first Temple by the Babylonians in 586BC. But as we shall see, it is not entirely out of the question that the Ark of the Covenant was recovered from the Temple ruins and that it was brought back to France – specifically to Chartres Cathedral.

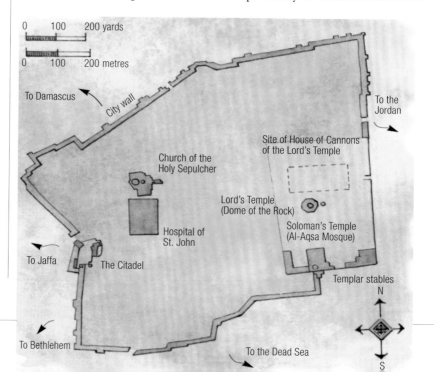

◀ The medieval Cathedral of Our Lady of Chartres is considered one of the finest examples of the French High Gothic style. The current cathedral, mostly constructed between 1193 and 1250, is one of at least five that have occupied the site since the town became a bishopric in the fourth century. The majority of the original stained glass windows survive intact, while the architecture has seen only minor changes since the early thirteenth century.

Speculation has also remained rife that the original Templars were recovering gold and silver objects that could easily have been hidden away in the labyrinth of tunnels beneath the Temple ahead of the destruction of 70 AD. This possibility began to appear more likely after the discovery of the Dead Sea Scrolls. This library of documents had been hidden in caves in the Jordan Valley around the same time as the Temple was destroyed in 70 AD. Among the scrolls found was one carefully detailing treasure that had been hidden beneath the Temple and in many other locations. This document is known as the "Copper Scroll." Is it possible that the Templars were in possession of an identical document and so therefore had more than a clue about where to search?

▼ February man warms his feet in the Zodiac window of Chartres Cathedral, which shows all the signs of the zodiac and the typical activity at that time of year. In addition to this there are two sculptured Zodiac/Labors of the Month cycles – one in the West Porch, the other in the North Porch.

Another possible explanation is that the Templars were looking for documents relating to those crucial years during which Christianity began to develop in the Holy Land, or scrolls relating to a much earlier period. Back in Champagne there were Jewish scholars, experts in ancient Hebrew, who would certainly have been able to translate anything the Templars might have found. Although there is no evidence that this actually took place, we do know that Jewish schools and almost certainly a Jewish university existed in Troyes. However, the role of any potential Hebrew translators in Champagne reviewing documents found in Jerusalem has to remain conjectural.

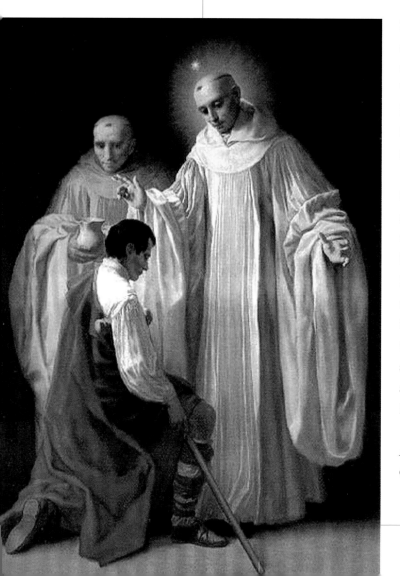

▼ St. Robert of Molesme welcomes St. Bernard of Clairvaux into the Cistercian Order. St. Robert was born ca.1027 in Troyes. He was canonized in 1222. A French Benedictine monk, abbot and monastic reformer, he was founder of Cîteaux (Latin Cistercium) Abbey (1098), which developed into the Cistercian Order.

St.ories of hidden treasure, lost artifacts and important documents have added significant excitement to studies of the Templars' hidden years, but there could be a series of more rational explanation for their virtual disappearance during this time.

Once the Templars were adopted as an accepted and authorized Roman Catholic institution, their real purpose becomes much easier to understand. It is possible that too many historical researchers have viewed the Templars in isolation and have failed to realize that they were, originally at least, only a part of something much bigger – something that was carefully planned in far-off Champagne.

Armed priests were an innovation to Christianity. It was almost certainly not a concept that would be readily accepted by many agencies within the Church. In the final analysis, it would take the authorization of a pope to declare the Templars to be an official body, and gaining the ear of the pontiff might be no easy task. What was required was a sympathetic pope and also people of influence who could argue the case for the holy army the Templars were intended to be.

Agencies within Champagne, and especially successive Champagne Counts themselves, were also gaining influence and laying plans in other directions during the decade the Templars remained silent in Jerusalem. When Hughes, former Count of Champagne, joined the Templar knights in 1125, his successor and nephew, Theobald II, immediately began to pour effort and money into increasing the size and importance of the Champagne Fairs.

▲ Bernard of Clairvaux, medieval reformer and mystic. He wrote the Rule for the order known as the Knights Templar, an order of men who took monastic vows and swore to defend the Holy Land militarily.

Most notable of all is that while the first Templar knights were somehow whiling away their time in Jerusalem, a young man of Champagne descent was steadily increasing his influence, both in France and with the popes of the period. His name was Bernard of Clairvaux and he is without doubt the most important person of the period in relation to the Templars when it comes to understanding the official creation of the Order that took place in 1129.

4

A new order of white monks

OUT OF CORRUPTION A NEW MONASTIC ORDER IS BORN

If the Templar Knights were ever to become a force to be reckoned with, they needed significant friends in high places. With the exception of the Knights of St. John (more commonly known as the Knights Hospitaller), who had developed from healers into soldiers, the concept of an order of fighting monks was a complete departure for the Roman Catholic world and many would view the concept with doubt and suspicion.

Only one man could sanction the Templar adventure and this was the pope – the unquestioned leader of the Catholic Church. In order to gain his sanction the Templars would have to ally themselves with some agency that was already flourishing and which had significant pull on the pope and his cardinals. It would certainly help if such an agency had close ties to Champagne, so that its aims and intentions would be similar to those of the Templars and it just so happened that such a body did exist in Champagne at the time – the Cistercians.

The monastic Cistercian order had come into existence in 1098, at a date coinciding almost exactly with the Christian capture of Jerusalem. The founding of the Cistercians was like those of other reformed orders of the time, partly a reaction against the laxity of many Benedictines, but was also born out of the religious zeal inspired by the First Crusade. The new order was created by Robert de Molesme, an aristocrat-turned-monk from Champagne. Robert was a man filled with reforming fervor who had tried to establish zealous new foundations on two occasions previously. Soon the Cistercian order became a monastic order like none that had ever existed before. The name "Cistercians" was probably derived from the "cisterns" or "baths" the monks employed in their first abbey. Alternatively it may have been associated with the word "Cistus," associated with a five-petalled rock rose named "Cistaceae" that is rich in medieval symbolism. This seems entirely possible, since the rose had a special part to play in the development of Champagne, where it was and still is grown commercially both for its perfume and its medicinal potential. The first abbey became known as "Cîteaux" and was located close to the northern border of Champagne and Burgundy. The name of the Cistercians does not derive from the place but rather the other way round.

No true understanding of the Knights Templar is possible without a grasp of the importance of the Cistercian monastic order and its shining star Bernard of Clairvaux.

Another young man from a leading aristocratic family with strong Champagne ties would quite quickly take over the Cistercian order lock, stock and barrel. His name was Bernard and he was set to become indisputably the most famous and influential monk and also statesman of his day. In 1113 he arrived at Cîteaux, which at the time was struggling to survive. Bernard, whose own father was a high-ranking noble who had fought with distinction in the First Crusade, brought with him to Cîteaux thirty relatives and friends. All became brothers at Cîteaux, and the fact that many of them were from aristocratic families also ensured potential support, gifts of land and money to the infant order.

Within three short years Bernard, still only twenty-three, set off north from Cîteaux to found a new abbey in Champagne, close to Troyes and on land granted by the Count of Champagne. This was the abbey of Clairvaux, after which Bernard is now known. Although the headquarters of the Cistercians remained the abbey of Cîteaux, it was to Bernard that bishops, cardinals, kings and even popes ultimately looked for guidance and advice. From the very start, Bernard had tremendous influence and he was the man who would carefully engineer the formation of the first Templar knights into a cohesive religious order that would be directly allied to the Cistercians.

It was to Bernard of Clairvaux that the Templars would look as their chief mentor, and they would still be sending prayers in his direction nearly two centuries later.

▶ The Knights Hospitaller was a Christian organisation that began as an Amalfitan hospital founded in Jerusalem in 1080, to provide care for poor, sick, or injured pilgrims to the Holy Land. After the Western Christian conquest of Jerusalem in 1099, during the First Crusade, it became a religious/military order under its own charter, and was charged with the care and defence of the Holy Land.

Corruption in high places

The laxity that existed within the Benedictine order of monks by the late eleventh century was due to the fact that the Benedictines had already been around for several centuries, during which time the Order's original ideals had been corrupted. The Order had been founded back in the sixth century, at which time St. Benedict of Nursia had laid out the rules necessary for a successful and pious monastic life.

Men and women had flocked from all parts of Europe and beyond to commit themselves to a life of poverty and prayer. By the eleventh century, there were dozens of Benedictine monasteries and convents, all of which were supported by charitable donations from society as a whole. The problem lay in the fact that many of the older Benedictine houses had become extremely rich, which led to corruption and laxity on behalf of those controlling the abbeys.

The original conception of St. Benedict had been that monks and nuns should live a life of contemplation, simplicity and physical work, but for those in the highest positions at least, this was no longer the case. Abbots had become lazy and indolent. They regularly became involved in politics, often took wives or mistresses, and lived opulent lifestyles that were far from Benedict's original conception.

With the new spiritual incentives of the eleventh and twelfth centuries – created in part by the call to crusade and a recognition that Christianity was under threat from Islam – and amidst a rising population, new recruits for the monastic life were not hard to find. But some of those entering the abbeys were educated men and they became less than satisfied with the direction the Benedictine order was taking. Such individuals were sworn

▼ St. Benedict of Nursia (ca.480–ca.547) is a Christian saint, honored by the Roman Catholic Church as the patron saint of Europe and students. Benedict's main achievement is his "Rule," containing precepts for his monks. The Rule of Benedict became one of the most influential religious rules in western Christendom. Benedict is often called the founder of western Christian monasticism.

to obedience, but this did not prevent a few radical monks from seeking to break away from the Benedictine order and start from scratch in abbeys where the rules of St. Benedict would be upheld to the letter. Such a man was Champagne-born Robert of Molesme.

Robert of Molesme was the younger son of one of the Count of Champagne's most trusted vassals, though we have no family name; Molesme is the name of the site where Robert's first abbey was founded. Tradition has it that Robert was born of a wealthy and influential Champagne family, and his literacy and intelligence bear witness to this. He was born around 1028 and at the age of fifteen he entered the Benedictine monastery of Montier-la-Celle, in Champagne.

By the year 1060 Robert had shown his intelligence and organizational skills to such an extent that he was made Abbot of the abbey of St. Michel-de-Tonnerre, also in Champagne. Robert became increasingly anxious about the laxity of the Benedictine order and eventually created a new abbey in Molesme. Unfortunately the new abbey grew quickly and quite soon began to show the same problems Robert had encountered elsewhere.

In desperation Robert eventually managed to gain ownership of some land just south of Champagne, in northern Burgundy. According to tradition this was granted to him by the Count of Champagne, though it is conceivable that this land was already associated with Robert's own family. He traveled there in 1098 and founded not just a new monastery but a whole new monastic order. It would become known as the Cistercian Order.

▲ St. Robert of Molesme (ca.1028–1111) was a Christian saint and abbot, one of the founders of the Cistercian Order in France. Robert was a member of the nobility in Champagne, who entered the abbey of Montier-la-Celle, near Troyes, at fifteen and later rose to the status of prior.

▲ An illumination of Stephen Harding (right) presenting a model of his church to the Blessed Virgin Mary. Cîteaux, c.1125. At this period Cistercian illumination was the most advanced in France, but within 25 years it was abandoned altogether under the influence of Bernard of Clairvaux.

▶ Cîteaux Abbey was founded in 1098 by a group of monks from Molesme Abbey, seeking to follow more closely the Rule of St Benedict, under the leadership of St Robert of Molesme, who became the first abbot. The great church of Cîteaux Abbey, begun in around 1140, was completed in 1193.

Robert of Molesme was determined from the start that the Cistercians should be radically different from their Benedictine counterparts. He envisaged a situation in which all monks, no matter what their rank, would engage in physical work as well as spending hours every day in church and keeping the necessary services. The new order would be self-sustaining and would not place its abbeys at the centre of towns and cities, as was the case with the Benedictine institutions. Cistercianism would alter radically as time went by, and in some cases abbeys would become just as corrupt and worldly as their Benedictine counterparts. However, in the early stages, the Cistercians were a radical departure and they proved to be extremely popular, especially to the younger sons of the lower and middle aristocracy, who traditionally looked towards the Church for their future. Not all the sons of the nobility could become knights and a zealous, reforming order such as the Cistercians provided an acceptable alternative.

The Cistercians did not have an auspicious start. Robert of Molesme was called back by the Pope to his former abbey of Molesme and the order fell under the guidance of the English-born Stephen Harding, who became the next abbot. As with the founding of many abbeys at the time, Cistercian writers make it plain that the monks at Cîteaux went through tremendous hardships in terms of hunger and general shortages in these early years. Thanks to the careful guidance of Stephen Harding, Cîteaux was somehow managing to survive, but the order needed a shot in the arm. This came in the form of a young man called Bernard.

Bernard was born of a very wealthy family in northern Burgundy, but was of partly Champagne ancestry. His father was called Tescelin, Lord of Fountaines, close to Dijon, and his mother was Aleth, daughter of a Champagne noble from Montbard. In 1113 Bernard arrived at the gates of Cîteaux Abbey with thirty of his relatives and retainers. All avowed their intention to become Cistercian monks. This sudden influx had an immediate bearing on the success of the Cistercian order, which from this point on grew quickly. Cîteaux eventually became the center of a vast number of abbeys and convents.

Just three years after his entry into the order, and while still only twenty-three years of age, Bernard was given land by Hughes, Count of Champagne, to found his own abbey of Clairvaux, just a few short kilometers (or a couple of miles) from Troyes. His influence began to grow rapidly, not only within the Cistercian Order, but also in the wider world beyond the monastery walls. By all accounts Bernard had tremendous charisma, but he was also of a high-born family and knew the right people. He corresponded with many of the great Church leaders of his day and gradually built up his influence. Most important of all, Bernard was a personal friend and a kinsman of the counts of Champagne, who themselves were growing in stature and influence at the time. Bernard soon had the ear of popes and he would go on to be the most influential church leader of his day. Bernard traveled extensively and made several trips to Rome. Despite the rural setting of his abbey at Clairvaux, people recognized him as both a mystic and a great reformer. Due to his tireless traveling and persuasion on at least two occasions, Bernard was in great part responsible for the election of a pope. These were Innocent II (pope from 1130 until 1143) and Eugene III (pope from 1145 until 1153). Before becoming pope as Bernardo Pignatelli, Eugene III had been a novice of Bernard at Clairvaux.

▲ St. Bernard holding a minuature of the Abbey of Clairvaux. St. Bernard was a Doctor of Marian devotion, the author of the Memorare; and a counsellor of Popes and Kings.

▼ The Cistercian Order originated towards the end of the eleventh century when certain monks broke away from the abbey of Molesme in Burgundy to follow a stricter rule. In a wild wood at Citeaux they built themselves a wooden monastery where other like-minded monks joined them.

Bernard of Clairvaux, as he would come to be called, though never the official leader of the Cistercian Order, was indisputably its most influential spokesman. As we have seen he became a pope maker and he also consorted with emperors, kings and princes. He was listened to by King Louis VI of France, was confident enough to remonstrate publicly with Guillaume X of Aquitaine and settled a dispute in 1137 between the Emperor Lothair and King Roger of Sicily. Bernard himself would become a saint within a few short years of his death in 1153 and was declared by the Pope in 1830 to be a Doctor of the Church. A Doctor of the Catholic Church is someone who had contributed greatly, especially in terms of theology and doctrine, and the distinction has only ever been granted to a very small number of individuals. Bernard of Clairvaux almost single-handedly laid the foundation for the new fighting monastic order that owed its existence to Champagne. In short, St. Bernard of Clairvaux took the idea of the Knights Templar and made it into a hard-and-fast reality.

It is unlikely that the idea for a fighting brotherhood of monks had come from Bernard himself, but it is highly likely that such an organization, especially based at Troyes in France, would have been seen by Bernard as a definite advantage in helping to secure the rights of the Church and in ultimately contributing to the prosperity of the region. With Bernard creating the list of rules, the Templars essentially became "Cistercians with swords." Like the Cistercians, they would be responsible only to the pope and could not be manipulated by secular leaders.

What went on behind the scenes we have no way of knowing, but just ahead of the Council of Troyes which ended early in 1129, Bernard corresponded with Hugues de Payen, leader of the Templars, who asked Bernard to write an order (list of rules) for the brotherhood. However, it should be remembered that Bernard was blood-tied to Hughes, formerly Count of Champagne, who was now a Templar, and also to André de Montbard, another of the original Templar knights. It is almost certain

▼ André de Montbard (ca.1103–1156) was the fifth Grand Master of the Knights Templar and also one of the new founders of the Order. The Montbard family came from Hochadel in Burgundy, and André was an uncle of St. Bernard of Clairvaux, being a half-brother of Bernard's mother Aleth de Montbard. He entered the Order in 1129 and went to Palestine, where he quickly rose to the rank of seneschal, deputy and second-in-command to the Grand Master.

that Bernard had been familiar with the ultimate intentions of the original knights for some years.

From the moment of their foundation, the Cistercians proved themselves to be innovative, intelligent and quite original. Unlike the Benedictines, the Cistercians, often also known as the "White Monks" because of their un-dyed woolen cowls, had two distinctly different types of monk. These were Choir Monks and Lay Brothers. All monks were expected to undertake manual labor but the Lay Brothers had special dispensation to live sometimes far from the abbey itself, which meant that land could be held and farmed at a considerable distance. This was a radical departure for monks and brought great flexibility to Cistercianism, as well as allowing any abbey to hold land in many different places, before eventually consolidating their holdings by buying, swapping or simply "acquiring" more land.

▲ The daily life of medieval monks was dedicated to worship, reading and manual labor, providing medical care for the community, educating the boys and novices, copying the manuscripts of classical authors and providing hospitality for pilgrims.

The order grew exponentially because as soon as circumstances allowed, a group of monks would leave an abbey to found a new house elsewhere. The Cistercians begged for wasteland, where nobody else wanted to live or farm. Using a variety of methods, they would enclose their land and eventually make it productive and profitable. In particular the Cistercians became adept at sheep rearing – a shrewd move at a time when as already observed, the need for wool was greater than it had ever been before. Sheep needed no extra feeding, could live almost anywhere and would gradually turn rough scrub into potential arable farmland.

The Cistercians were also democratic and in this respect, because of the structure of the organization, they were quite unique. All leaders were voted into office by the monks themselves and any could be relieved of their position if they failed the order. Each new abbey became a daughter house of the abbey from which it had been founded. National frontiers were no obstacle to the Cistercians, who soon had abbeys all over Europe. The same was broadly true of the Benedictines, but in the case of the Cistercians, the ties to the ultimate mother abbey at Cîteaux were much closer. Meetings were held regularly at mother houses and once each year at Cîteaux for all the abbots in the Cistercian family.

The rules of the order were strictly observed. They had been laid down by St.ephen Harding but were altered by Bernard of Clairvaux to suit changing circumstances. Nowhere was the influence of the Cistercian order felt more keenly than in Champagne, where Bernard regularly met with the Count and his advisors. Champagne had many Cistercian monasteries and these were mother houses to a vast array of monasteries in other countries. Ultimately, Clairvaux had the most daughter houses, many of which had daughter houses of their own. Thus the overall influence of the area in terms of Cistercianism was pronounced. But, at the same time, Bernard of Clairvaux was becoming an astute politician whose influence with crowned heads and cardinals led to the adoption of the disputed Pope Innocent II in 1130. Around this time there were often arguments regarding the election of a new pope, and men who would eventually be known as "antipopes" were common. However, it was two years before this, in 1128, that a great Catholic Council was held in Troyes, Champagne. The Council of Troyes was called by the Pope and, like other councils of the sort, was a way for both Church and secular leaders to come together in order to thrash out problems that had developed throughout the Catholic world. It was here that Bernard of Clairvaux's influence would truly make itself felt – he prevailed upon Pope Honorius II to accept the Knights Templar as an officially sanctioned monastic order.

▼ The rule that was established at the Council of Troyes was relatively compact. It contained only 72 articles, which mainly set out the rules in relation to monastic life of the Knights Templar. It contained general rules that could also apply in monasteries of different religious Orders. These included vows of obedience, poverty and chastity, rules on communal life.

A cohesive plan?

As host to the Council of Troyes, which brought spiritual and secular leaders to Champagne from the four corners of Roman Catholic Christendom, the Count of Champagne would have had significant influence. Bernard of Clairvaux was not only close to the Count in terms of the distance between his abbey and Troyes, he was directly related to the man (a cousin on his mother's side). No pope would refuse any reasonable request from such a generous host as Count Theobald II, who was a great patron of the Church, as well as being a very influential statesman and a powerful ruler. In any case, Bernard of Clairvaux put forward a case for the Templars that must have looked very attractive.

If the order was formed, Bernard suggested, it would become virtually a private army and one dedicated absolutely to the pope. No other secular or spiritual leader would be able to command the Knights Templar, who would be responsive only to the pope's authority. Since popes at the time were never secure in their office, this incentive alone must have looked very attractive. Like secular leaders in times of war, popes had to enlist the support of their own nobles or groups of mercenary soldiers. They were often subjected to intimidation from antipopes or those whose kingdoms surrounded the papal states in Italy.

It is almost certain that discussions regarding the Templars had been taking place for some time between Bernard of Clairvaux and the Pope, because Hugues de Payens and his companions had returned from Jerusalem to attend the Council of Troyes, a journey

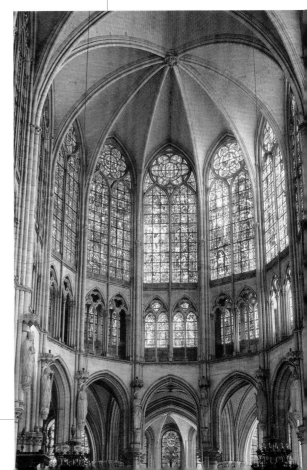

▼ The Cathedral of St. Peter and St. Paul in Troyes. Work began on this jewel of Gothic architecture in 1200 and continued until the middle of the sixteenth century. Troyes was the capital city of the region of Champagne, center of the Cistercian Order and home of Hugues de Payens.

▲ Around 1119, two veterans of the First Crusade (Hugues de Payens and his relative Godfrey de Saint-Omer) proposed the creation of a monastic order for the protection of the pilgrims that attempted the journey from the coastline at Jaffa into the Holy Land. Their emblem was of two knights riding on a single horse, emphasizing the Order's poverty.

that would have taken many weeks. That these first Templars should have found their way back to Troyes at precisely the same time as the Council was convened there by mere chance is beyond belief. There, amidst great pomp and ceremony, the Poor Knights of Christ and the Temple of Solomon were sanctioned as an official monastic order and granted the right to bear arms against all enemies of Christianity. From the outset they would live by a set of rules converted by Bernard of Clairvaux from the rules by which the Cistercians were governed.

It is impossible to say for certain that there was a direct and deliberate link between the creation of the Cistercian order, the rise of the Champagne Fairs and the establishment of the Knights Templar. However, it appears that all of these happenings were destined to serve the same objective – namely the prosperity, power and economic growth of the region. Certainly none of these events worked against the best interests of Champagne or its rulers, and it seems likely that there was indeed a connection, discussed and planned over decades in the dark confines of the Count's palace in Troyes.

Whether or not this was the case, the first Knights Templar wasted no time at all – which is especially surprizing considering they had seemingly achieved nothing for over a decade. Even before the Council members were leaving Champagne, Hugues de Payen and his companions were mounted and off on a huge recruitment campaign. And before St. Bernard of Clairvaux can be cleared of any self-interest in his association with the infant Knights Templar, it should be remembered that the second original Templar knight, André de Montbard, was his uncle. Bernard was blood-tied to Hughes, former Count of Champagne, and was probably also related to Hugues de Payen.

◀ The west side of the Dome of the Rock, Jerusalem, also known as the al-Aqsa Mosque, believed to be built on the site of Solomon's Temple. The Templars made part of this building their headquarters during the twelfth century.

◀ Early Templars in battle dress. Two knights were often shown on one horse to signify their vow of poverty.

5

An official order of fighting knights

A PAPAL EDICT AND RULES FOR A HOLY WARRIOR'S LIFE

t was probably not at all difficult for Bernard of Clairvaux to convince Pope Honorius II that everyone could gain from a monastic order dedicated to fighting the enemies of Christianity. Popes at the time were not without significant enemies. There were frequent schisms within the Church and a series of antipopes arose at this time to make life even more difficult for the pontiff. On several occasions during the period, alternative candidates were proposed when a pope died. If one such individual did not back down and each had his own support from different political factions or parts of the Church, two potential popes existed, sometimes for years at a time. The thought of having a powerful private army that responded only to the will of the pope must have seemed very comforting. Of course, nine knights did not constitute an army, but the Cistercian movement was growing exponentially, so there was no reason to believe that the same would not be true of the prospective Knights Templar.

Things were not going particularly well in the Holy Land either. Although King Baldwin II had achieved a degree of success during his reign in Jerusalem, between 1118 and 1131, life there was never settled or easy, partly because of pressure from surrounding Muslim states, but also on account of Christian political

◀ Baldwin II had no male heirs but had already designated his daughter Melisende to succeed him. Baldwin II wanted to safeguard his daughter's inheritance by marrying her to a powerful lord. Fulk I, a wealthy crusader and experienced military commander, married Melisende in 1129. Fulk and Melisende became joint rulers of Jerusalem in 1131 following Baldwin II's death.

fighting, which sometimes led to Christians being involved in open conflict with other Christians. In 1129, King Baldwin had sought to strengthen the Christian position in the Holy Land by capturing Damascus, but had singularly failed to do so. The Muslim threat existed on all sides, but most of the really powerful Western magnates who had contributed to the First Crusade had left the area years before. The region was garrisoned in the main by Western aristocrats who had stayed in the hope of securing land and power, together with their personal entourages. Meanwhile kings and princes who had been present at the First Crusade could not afford to keep vast armies in the field indefinitely.

Keeping infantry and archers in the Holy Land, let alone armed knights with retinues and numbers of warhorses, was prohibitively expensive. By the reign of King Baldwin II there were some aristocratic families living in the Near East, but the numbers of Christians present were nowhere near matching the hundreds of thousands of Muslims surrounding them. Kings and great lords in far-off countries could not afford to keep armies present and provisioned thousands of miles away, no matter how much they may have wished to do so.

In addition to the embattled Christian forces in the Near East, another incentive to the Pope for sanctioning an order such as that of the Knights Templar answered a problem that had existed for decades. As had been the case prior to the fighting of the First Crusade, successive popes must have wondered what to do with all the hot-headed younger sons of great and lesser lords who had little to do in Europe except to cause trouble for the Church and society as a whole.

For Honorius II, there was probably no doubt at all that military orders such as the Knights Templar and the developing Knights Hospitaller were the way forward, both as a way of adding to depleted forces in and around Jerusalem, and in terms of adding to his own personal security and power. The Pope had nothing to lose and everything to gain

In Praise of the New Knighthood

Bernard of Clairvaux did have one major obstacle to overcome in terms of convincing the Pope that the idea of a military army was acceptable in Christian terms. Many Christians at the time were very devout and tried to live by the letter of the scriptures. These forbade Christians from bearing arms against others, and to many people the thought of a monk killing and maiming anyone was repugnant.

▼ St. Bernard (1090–1153), teaching in a Dominican monastery, from a French manuscript of 1420–81. In his document, *In Praise of the New Knighthood*, Bernard of Clairvaux voiced his view of knights, warfare and the conquest of the Holy Land.

To deal with this problem, Bernard wrote what amounted to an open letter, though it was specifically addressed to Hugues de Payen, who would become the first Grand Master of the Templar Order. The document was entitled *In Praise of the New Knighthood*. It is clear from the nature of Bernard's words that this document was intended to be an explanation, an apology and an aid to recruitment.

Bernard commenced the open letter by taking the aristocratic knights of his day to task. He accused them of being cruel, vain, worldly and even effeminate. He suggested that for all their gold spurs, painted shields and gaudy colors, these "temporal" knights invariably fought for worldly ends and that for their misdeeds and greed, they could expect to go to Hell.

He then extolled the virtues of knights who he suggested had effectively been monks from the beginning of their stay in Jerusalem; he praised their

 The Templar Order followed strict religious rules, The Rule of Benedict, and as such conducted their daily lives much as monks would have done, hence being known as "Warrior Monks." The knights wore a white surcoat with a red cross and a white mantle; the sergeants wore a black tunic with a red cross on front and back and a black or brown mantle. The white mantle was assigned to the Templars at the Council of Troyes in 1129 and was a symbol of religious purity and the fact they had entered a life of celibacy. There was a cardinal rule that the warriors of the Order should never surrender unless the Templar flag had fallen. This uncompromising principle, along with their reputation for courage, excellent training and heavy armament, made the Templars one of the most feared combat forces in medieval times.

modesty, their lack of ornamentation and their general demeanor. Using scriptural passages from the Bible, Bernard composed a masterful piece of Christian propaganda. "Of course," he suggested, "it was wrong to kill anyone if any other course of action proved to be possible," but since any belief or lifestyle that was not Christian was, by implication, inherently evil, killing Muslims who would not convert could hardly be construed as a sin.

▶ Each Templar knight was allowed three horses and a squire – three horses would have been a great expense at the time but as they were used solely for military purposes it was not deemed an extravagance. However, they could have no gold, silver or ornamental trappings.

▼ Bronze coin of Baldwin II, King of Jerusalem (1118–31) and benefactor of the Knights Templar, depicting him wearing chain mail and conical helmet.

Bernard also extolled the virtues of a Jerusalem "rescued" from the hands of those he referred to as "pagans." He suggested that the Holy City had been "stolen" – as if Christians alone had any right to inhabit and control it.

Within his document *In Praise of the New Knighthood*, Bernard of Clairvaux began to put forward some of his ideas as to how the Templars should dress and act. He suggested that the new knights should have short hair and plain clothes. He insisted that they should refrain from ornamentation in the case of their own appearance or that of their horses. Indeed he suggested that they should abstain from washing and should consider their threadbare state to be a virtue. Horses should be picked by holy knights for their strength and speed, but never for their magnificence. Armor and equipment should be strong and effective, but never created to look brash or opulent. Soldier monks should be modest and kind to fellow Christians, they must never be haughty or vain and, most important of all, rather than fearing death in battle they should welcome it because, as Bernard said, it meant they would be going directly to paradise.

It is possible to see in the words of Bernard of Clairvaux the first stirrings of something that would gain tremendous importance in the years that followed. This was the concept of "chivalry," which was, in part at least, the application of force – even deadly force, but used for good. In time the concept of chivalry would become a virtual obsession within Western European society and the concept of the "peerless knight" would dominate literature and fund aristocratic behavior.

▲ A nineteenth-century engraving of an armed Templar in combat on his rearing horse, both in battle dress.

From the very outset there was a sort of mysticism attached to knights who forsook all the temptations of the world in order to strive for the good of Christian values and to defend the weak. It is easy to see how the average well-born youth of this period might have been heavily influenced by Bernard's words. The desire to "fight for the right" was appealing because in the mind of would-be Templars it meant adventure, armed warfare but also dispensation from the responsibility of becoming a heavily armed killer. For younger sons of aristocrats, the Church represented one of the very few options for their future lives. Being part of a military order such as the Templars meant following a career in the Church and yet utilizing all the skills most of them had been learning from the cradle.

The Rule of Conduct

All monastic orders had a Rule of Conduct, which amounted to a carefully created series of instructions that monks were expected to follow to the letter. The new Knights Templar would be no exception and Bernard of Clairvaux clearly associated the Templars with his own order, the Cistercians. Rather than starting from scratch with a Rule of Conduct for the Templars, Bernard based it specifically on that which was working so well for the Cistercians, who by this time were spreading rapidly throughout Europe.

▼ St. Bernard of Clairvaux was canonized 21 years after his death in 1174 and his skull was placed in Troyes Cathedral. The skull was taken to Switzerlan for safety during the French Revolution.

Of course there had to be differences, because Cistercian monks were forbidden, except under specific circumstances, from traveling beyond the holdings of their own abbey. Dietary considerations would also differ because at this time Cistercian monks were strict vegetarians, whereas the extra physical effort necessary for soldiers and knights demanded a meat-rich diet.

Templar knights would also be allowed, and even encouraged, to let their beards grow, but according to the Primitive Rule of the Templars they were still committed to the tonsure of monks. This hairstyle set monks apart from other members of society and involved shaving a part of the top of the head. Templar monks would be expected to take part in regular church services, but not to the same extent as Cistercian brothers, though they would take vows of poverty, chastity and celibacy. During times when there was fighting to be done, the knights themselves would not be expected to work alongside other members of the Order, whose duties would be to serve the knights and to enable the Order to flourish and grow, but neither were they expected to live lives of ease in between battles. On the contrary, they were instructed to keep their weapons and equipment in good order and to participate cheerfully in anything that was required of them.

In today's terms the prospect of becoming a Templar knight may not seem inviting. They would often be fighting in hot and dusty places, could never benefit from the spoils of war and must never retreat unless outnumbered by the enemy by at least three to one. However, life during the period was generally hard and unremitting, and the spiritual incentives to become a "knight for God" must have added to the thirst for adventure that was common to young men of noble families.

From the outset the name of the new order would be "The Poor Knights of Christ and the Temple of Solomon." This implied that the personnel in the Order would have no money or possessions of their own. Everything each individual owned was given to the Order at the time they joined, but this alone would not fund what would turn out to be a very expensive enterprise.

Every man, horse and piece of equipment necessary to fight the pagans, wherever that fight might take place, had to be brought from Western Europe by land and sea to the field of battle. This alone was a prohibitively expensive undertaking. Each knight would require a massive infrastructure in order to support him in battle and the Templar Order would go

▲ The monastic tonsure was a symbol of the monks' renunciation of worldly fashion and esteem. A tonsure might also indicate that a monk had received clerical status.

▲ Blacksmith monk, illuminated initial from St. Gregory the Great's "Moralia in Job," manuscript of the Abbey of Saint-Pierre at Préaux, eleventh to twelfth century.

▼ Coins of the Knights Templar, France, 1285–1290 AD. A small hoard of silver deniers of King Philip IV "The Fair" and Louis IX (1226–1270 AD). The coins depict a cross and castle. Each measures about 18–20 mm diameter and weighs around 1 gram.

on to have perhaps fifty, sixty, seventy or more personnel for every individual who ever lifted a sword. This did not include only personal attendants but a host of others such as blacksmiths, engineers, cooks, supporting foot soldiers and more, actually present where the Templar was garrisoned. In addition a Templar knight was supported by farmers, horse breeders, sailors, merchants and innumerable others back in France or in any of the regions where the Templars ultimately had holdings.

Only by convincing society as a whole that the enterprise was a worthy and noble one could the Templars hope to receive the gifts of land and money that would be necessary in order to fund their objectives. It was therefore important from the outset to "fly the flag," which is why documents such as Bernard of Clairvaux's *In Praise of the New Knighthood* would prove to be so important.

But the Templars had great teachers. The Cistercians had already made self-sufficiency into an art form. The Templars would go on to employ the very same tactics. At the same time they were in a potentially more fortunate position than their Cistercian brothers, because they could travel wherever was needed and were not tied to a specific location. From the outset it was obvious that they would have to farm, trade and use any means at their disposal to get ever more knights and foot soldiers fighting in the Holy Land.

Grand Masters of the Knights Templar

probable coats of arms

Hugues de Paynes
1118-1136

Robert de Craon
1136-1149

Everard des Barres
1149-1152

Bernard de Tremelay
1152-1153

Andre de Montbard
1153-1156

Bertrand de Blanquefort
1156-1169

Philip de Milly of Nablus
1169-1171

Odo de St Amand
1171-1180

Arnold de Torroja
1180-1185

Gerard de Ridefort
1185-1189

Robert de Sable
1191-1193

Gilbert Erail
1194-1200

Philip de Plessiez
1201-1209

William de Chartres
1210-1219

Peter de Montaigu
1219-1232

Armand de Perigord
1232-1244

Richard de Bures
1244-1247

William de Sonnac
1247-1250

Reynald de Vichiers
1250-1256

Thomas Berard
1256-1273

William de Beaujeu
1273-1291

Theobald Gaudin
1291-1293

Jacques de Molay
1293-1314

◀ Speculative representation of the arms of the Grand Masters, the leaders of the Knights Templar. The Grand Master was the spiritual, political and military leader of the Order. He was chosen by a complex electoral system similar to that used in Venice to elect the Doge. The Grand Master was supposed to be beyond the influence of kings, and to answer only to the Pope. The Grand Master presided from Jerusalem, and subsequently from Acre (and from Cyprus in the final years). He was normally installed for life, though there was precedent for a Grand Master resigning. He in theory ruled with the advice of a council, the Chapter, and important decisions were usually made at chapter meetings. The list of Templar Grand Masters begins with Hugues de Payens (1118–1136/7) and ends with Jacques de Molay (1293–1314). There were twenty one other Masters.

A complex infrastructure would be necessary if the enterprise was to succeed and that meant having skilled commanders who were as much "managers" as generals. They would be headed by a Grand Master. Though the origin of the title is somewhat obscure, Hugues de Payens is first referred to in this way at the Council of Troyes in 1129. He appears to have been a very shrewd operator and defined what this particular position needed to be, so that the Order could continue to flourish in the years to come.

After a decade of apparent inactivity, the Council of Troyes set the seal on the Templar undertaking. It has been suggested, by speculative writers on the subject, that the money necessary to fund the beginning of the Templar Order may have come from treasures of one sort or another that the original Templar knights had discovered in Jerusalem. It is a tempting thought but probably was not the case. After all, the Cistercian order began with nothing and within a decade or two was successful beyond anyone's expectations. What is more, the Templars had good teachers, whereas the Cistercians had learned their lessons from scratch. And when it came to prizing gifts of land and money from the inhabitants of Western Europe, the Templars soon became experts.

Not everyone could personally travel to take part in the crusade against the Muslims, but giving freely to organizations such as the Templars was seen as a way to gain favor with the Almighty. The Church offered dispensations for those who offered such gifts and, in this period, people were credulous and genuinely did believe that such dispensations would be worth something when Purgatory beckoned.

But the gifts alone would not be enough. The Templars needed to take what they could get from people rich or poor and then use it in such a way that it would grow. This strategy would turn out to be the genius of the Templar movement.

▶ Prince Richard I of Capua making a donation to the Abbey of St. Angelo in Formis, from a twelfth-century manuscript. This shows the regular practice of making donations to monasteries and churches during the Middle Ages.

6

Monks at home and at war

THE EXPANSION OF AN ORDER FROM TROYES TO PARIS AND ONWARDS

From almost the moment that the adoption of the Templars as an approved Roman Catholic institution was accepted by the Council of Troyes, Hugues de Payen and his trusted brothers set out to spread the name of the Templars far and wide.

Gifts of money and land flowed in from all directions, especially from landed aristocrats, because it seemed as though everyone applauded the ideals of the Templars and wanted to support their defense of Christianity far from the shores of the West. However, it might be incorrect to assume that nothing had been achieved in terms of starting the Templar adventure prior to the Council of Troyes. For example, there is good evidence that significant holdings had already been granted to the Templars by the kings of England and Scotland some time before the Council of Troyes took place. The first meeting between King David I of Scotland and Hugues de Payen is documented as having taken place in 1128, whereas the Council of Troyes that made the Templars an official order did not take place until 1129. It is likely that land grants, especially in Midlothian, were made at this time. There is some conjecture that Hugues also met the English king during the same visit to Britain. What really makes the notion of the Templars already owning land in Britain prior to 1129 believable, is the speed with which they began to exploit holdings in Britain after the Council of Troyes. It is very likely that the discussions at the Council were merely a way of regularizing and putting a signature to decisions that had already been made.

◀ Knights Templar chapel and tomb in Laon, France. The chapel was built around 1180, serving the local commandery. Following the dissolution of the Order, the property was transferred to the Knights of St. John (the Hospitallers). While there are several round or octagonal churches in France, only three of them were actually built by the Templars.

From the lines of the Primitive Rule of the Templars, which represented the general rules by which Templar personnel should live and work, it is obvious that great thought had gone into ensuring that everything that took place within Templarism would be for the good of the Order as a whole. From the outset, Templarism ran like a well-oiled machine and nobody, from the humblest squire to the most elevated master, was in any doubt as to how to behave under any given circumstance.

Templarism relied from the outset on "preceptories," which were communities of Templar knights and their attendants that fulfilled more or less the same role as a monastic abbey. Although the spiritual heart of Templarism remained in Troyes, Champagne, the headquarters of the order would eventually be in Paris. It was to Paris that masters of the different regions and preceptories would travel on a regular basis to deal with matters that had a bearing on Templarism. This was because so much of the area we now know as France, nominally or in fact, lay within the overall control of the French Crown. Paris would eventually become the richest and most opulent of all the Templar holdings – which in part would eventually spell trouble for the Order.

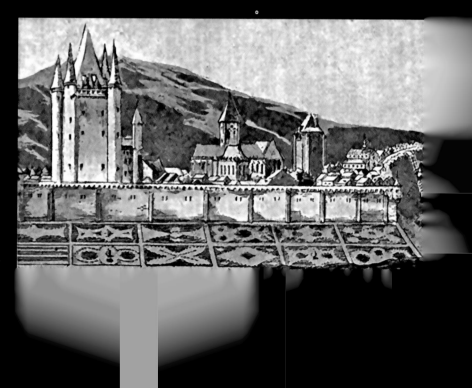

Knights Templar Palace in Paris, France. Many Templars in France were killed under the authority of King Philip. Other monarchs in Europe followed suit; even if they weren't jealous of Templar power, the opportunity to acquire their lands was too good to pass up. Some Templars were taken in by other monastic military orders, like the Hospitallers. A few escaped to areas outside papal control, like Scotland, which was at the time under excommunication. Most simply disappeared; their

Acquisition of land

The Templars could achieve little in terms of their first objective of fighting Muslims in the Holy Land until they had acquired enough land and money to fund their first expeditionary force. It was for this reason that Hugues de Payen and his companions set off on a protracted journey of recruitment and information. Their first journey was to England, Wales and Scotland, followed by a long circuit around the more powerful kingdoms in Western Europe. Everyone apparently wished to contribute to the new order and it wasn't long before local preceptories were being established in dozens of locations.

A preceptory might be the center of extensive farm holdings, or a regional headquarters in a large town or city. In terms of daily life, it was run in a very similar way to a Cistercian abbey. The preceptory would be centerd around a church, where prayers and services would be held on a regular basis each day. It would also have a refectory, where the personnel would gather to eat, and a chapter house, where the fully fledged Templar brothers would gather each day in order to make decisions regarding the running of the preceptory.

▶ Templar Church of St. Michael, Garway, just north of Monmouth. Garway is well known as a templar preceptory. The small Church of St. Michael sitting in the Monnow Valley is all that remains from the original preceptory. On 16 July 1199 the Knight's Templar received confirmation from King John that the gift of 2,000 acres of land at Garway officially belonged to the Order.

◀ The Templars used at least three types of horses. The "destrier" was used by the knights. The "palefroi" horse was used by the dames and the churchmen. The "roncin" was a strong horse used for farm work. The areas of Aragon, Castille and Gascony were some of the main sources for Templar horses; from there, they were exported to the rest of France, England and the Holy Land.

Once a preceptory was established in a certain location, efforts would be made to increase and consolidate Templar holdings in and around this. Much of what the Templars would achieve relied heavily on farming. The Order would go on to raise its own horses, of which it needed literally thousands, for battle, general transport and agriculture, but farms could also be profitable for selling produce into the open market and for growing food for the community.

▼ Harvesting (ca.1190). Before planting seeds it is necessary to break down the earth. Poor farmers who could not borrow or hire a plough had to use a spade for this work. The spade was made of wood with iron shoes to protect it from wearing out. It was used for preparing the ground, especially on the croft and also for digging ditches when draining land.

Like the Cistercians, the Templars would be an essentially democratic institution. Masters and grand masters would be voted into office at Chapter. This was the name given to the regular meetings that all fully fledged Templar brothers attended. There decisions would be made regarding the running of any particular preceptory, and ultimately of the Order as a whole. These were held in every Templar preceptory on a regular basis, where decisions would also be made regarding newcomers, as well as plans for dealing with the injured, sick and the elderly.

▲ Meeting of Chapter of the Knights Templar in Paris on 22 April 1147. The meeting was organized by Robert the Burgundian, in the presence of Louis VII of France and Pope Eugene III.

Although the spiritual heart of Templarism remained in Troyes, Champagne, the headquarters of the Order would eventually be in Paris. It was to Paris that masters of the different regions and preceptories would travel to form a higher chapter, designed to deal with matters that had a bearing on the rapidly growing Templar family of properties. The choice of Paris, as opposed to Troyes, was politically expedient. For one thing, the counts of Champagne were often at odds with the French Crown, and French kings would probably have taken exception to the generals of what amounted to a "private army" meeting in Troyes. If such meetings were held in Paris, the French Crown could see what was happening and be certain that nothing prejudicial to the good of French interests was taking place.

As we will presently see, no other monastic institution would have as much influence on the development of Europe as that of the Knights Templar. They would go on to create a vast empire of wealth and influence, but it all had to start somewhere, and it commenced with a begging bowl.

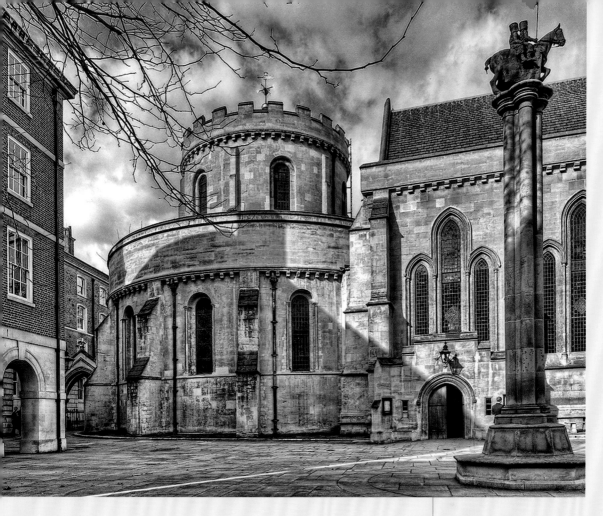

▲ The Round Church that presently lies in the heart of London's legal district was not the original location of the Templar community in London. They had earlier been located in the High Holborn district, but the expansion of the Order at the end of the twelfth century saw the need to move to larger facilities. This was a common trend throughout Europe as the Order expanded as their popularity in Christendom grew. Only four round churches now survive in England. They are the Temple Church in London, Little Maplestead in Essex, St. Sepulcher's in Northampton and Holy Sepulcher in Cambridge.

There is strong circumstantial evidence that the Templar Order was up and running for some time before the decision of the Pope at the Council of Troyes in 1128–29 made the Order into an officially sanctioned Roman Catholic body. Although there is little in the way of documentation to substantiate the claim, it is generally accepted among Templar historians that in April of 1128, Hugues de Payen and André de Montbard (Bernard of Clairvaux's uncle) visited King Henry I of England and that they received from him significant grants of property – in particular a site at Holborn, London that would house England's Templar headquarters.

▲ King David I of Scotland knighting a squire. David was one of medieval Scotland's greatest monastic patrons. In 1113, in perhaps his first act as Prince of the Cumbrians, he founded Selkirk Abbey for the Tironensians. David founded more than a dozen new monasteries in his reign. These new monasteries, and the Cistercian ones in particular, introduced new agricultural practices. Cistercian labor, for instance, transformed southern Scotland into one of northern Europe's most important sources of sheep wool.

It is also reported that Hugues and André took the opportunity in the same year to pay a visit to King David I of Scotland, where they were also received cordially and given gifts of land. Can we see in this behavior simple prior planning or a deliberate fait accompli? Bernard of Clairvaux was already on extremely good terms with both the English and Scottish kings, with whom he had communicated about creating new Cistercian abbeys in both England and Scotland, so doubtless his influence was critical in these initial stages.

If powerful kings were already supporting the Templars before the Council of Troyes took place, then would the Pope have had any chance of refusing to sanction the Order? It was extremely important for the Pope, who was utterly dependent on the support of national rulers throughout the Catholic world, to listen to what they had to say and to carry favor with them if at all possible. Templarism appealed to both the populace and its rulers, a fact that the Pope could not have failed to recognize. In this, as in many other situations right up until the disaster that struck the Templars in 1307, those at its helm often seemed to be one step ahead of the political game.

There is a persistent legend that at the time the Templars were founded, their leader, Hugues de Payen, was a married man. And though we do not know whether any of his colleagues were married, it has to be a distinct possibility. This might have proved to be something of an embarrassment to the leader of an order that was based in part of celibacy. However, such a situation was dealt with in the Primitive Rule of the Templars. Married men could become Templars, though in the initial stages of the Order, at least, they would not be allowed to wear the white mantle of the Templars. If a married Templar died, half his family property would go to his wife and half would be bequeathed to the Templars.

Hugues is said to have been married to a rich Scottish heiress named Catherine de St. Clair, though there is no positive proof that this was the case, and the suggestion is of fairly recent French origin and likely to be unreliable. It is further suggested that a year before the Council of Troyes, the Templars received significant holdings from Katherine's family in Scotland at the place then known as "Balantrodoch," not far from Edinburgh. Although the truth of the story cannot be verified, it is a fact that the Templars did have land in this location, and to this day there is a village in this location called "Temple." The ruins of Templar buildings and a later Knights Hospitaller chapel still exist within the village. The St. Clair, later Sinclair, family would become significant to the Templar story at a much later date. However, there may be no St. Clair (Sinclair) connection at such an early date,- and this land could easily have come to the Templars during the visit they made to Scotland in 1128, a year prior to the Council of Troyes.

▼ Roofless church of the Knights Templar in Temple (Balantrodoch), former seat of the Knights Templar. In 1127, Hugues de Payens, the first Grand Master met with David I in Scotland, and was granted the lands of Balantrodach. Balantrodach became their principal Templar seat and Preceptory in Scotland until the suppression of the order between 1307 and 1312.

Defined by the Rule

It is obvious from the open letter Bernard of Clairvaux wrote to Hugues de Payen and the Primitive Rule of the Templars, which must have taken some time to construct, that before the Council of Troyes was convened and the Templars were formerly introduced, every possible contingency had been dealt with. The Templars were riding in the wake of the Cistercians, who by 1128 had already existed for some time, so it made sense for the Templars to learn at the very start from any possible mistakes that had been made in early Cistercianism. It is thanks to the Primitive Rule of the Templars that we know so much about the daily life and circumstances of the average Templar knight.

Each knight would be in possession of three horses, any of which could be substituted at the behest of the Master. A knight was also supplied with all the tack and metalware necessary to equip himself and his steed. He would be given all required armaments, though it was his responsibility to look after his equipment and keep it in good condition. This would include a sword, which at the time would have been prohibitively expensive (probably costing the equivalent of a luxury car today). Like all knights of the period, the Templar knight would have a squire. It was the squire's job to assist the knight in every way possible. He would generally be a young man, and perhaps someone who intended eventually to become a Templar knight himself.

There were very strict rules about the way the Templars would live. For example, it was stated quite plainly that Templars, though sleeping in common dormitories, would retire fully clothed (including their shoes) and that a light should be kept burning at all times. The Rule makes it plain that this last requirement was to ensure that no knight could ever be subsequently accused of sexual misconduct.

▼ The three extant medieval manuscripts comprise the Primitive Rule, Hierarchical St.atutes, Penances, Conventual Life, the Holding of Ordinary Chapters, Further Details on Penances, and Reception into the Order, formalizing the exceptional combination of soldier and monk. The Rule evolved over almost 150 years of the Order's history.

The Templar knight, and indeed all Templar personnel, would be supplied with all necessary clothing. If he was fighting in a hot climate he would be allowed to wear a linen shirt, though under all other circumstances it would be made of wool. Only fully trained knights would be allowed to wear the white mantle that made the Templars so famous. Like the habit of the Cistercians this would originally have been made from un-dyed wool. The red cross that all Templars eventually bore on their mantle did not form part of the original uniform. This cross was considered to be a symbol of martyrdom and the Templars were granted the right to wear it by Pope Eugene III in 1147 when he issued a Papal bull regarding the matter. (Pope Eugene III, who reigned from 1145 to 1153, had originally been a novice at the Abbey of Clairvaux, under Bernard of Clairvaux.)

The rule of the Cistercians, adopted almost entirely by the Templars, was quite appropriate for a fighting force. All monks were, in principle at least, extremely disciplined. Like the monks they truly were, the Templars were expected to be modest, to accept humbly what they were given and to follow without question the decisions of those who had been voted into positions of authority.

▼ The abbey of Rievaulx was founded in 1132. It was built to be the first Cistercian outpost in the North, an abbey from which the White Monks could reform and colonize northern England and Scotland. The abbey attracted recruits from near and far, as well as high-profile benefactors such as Henry II (1135–1154) and King David of Scotland (1124–1153). The monks' dormitory at Rievaulx accommodated about 140 monks.

▲ There was a threefold division of the ranks of the Templars: the aristocratic knights, the lower-born sergeants and the clergy. Knights were required to be of knightly descent and to wear white mantles. Beneath the knights and drawn from lower social strata were the sergeants. They were either equipped as light cavalry with a single horse or served in other ways such as administering the property of the Order or performing menial tasks and trades. Chaplains, constituting a third Templar class, were ordained priests who saw to the Templars' spiritual needs.

Although not taking a vow of silence, Templars were instructed to keep talk to an absolute minimum and never to indulge in idle chatter. During meals they would listen to parts of the scriptures being read to them and there were even extensive rules concerning diet. From the creation of the Templars, meat would only be served three times a week, and on certain feast days. The Rule made it plain that to eat meat was considered a sin, but it was allowed on the grounds that Templars needed to remain strong and fit. On all other days only vegetables would be served, though the dietary rules of the Templars were not at all out of the ordinary for the period. At least Templar personnel could be sure of eating on a regular basis, which was not uniformly the case among the public.

As well as knights and squires, we know of the Templar rank "Sergeant at arms' and the Templars were also composed of foot soldiers, farmers, tanners, blacksmiths, stonemasons and, in fact, men from every trade necessary to make the Order as efficient and self-sufficient as possible. Women were definitely not allowed anywhere near a Templar preceptory and it was made plain in the Rule that the fairer sex were viewed with great suspicion.

Punishment

Templar knights, and in fact all Templar personnel, were expected to behave in a seemly manner. However, most of the knights came from the aristocracy and so had been brought up in families that were sometimes very powerful. This meant that they were used to having their own way and, more to the point, having others do their bidding. This would not be possible within the Order and doubtless it took some time for new Templars to adjust.

Templars in battle were known for their heroic prowess, chivalry, courage and discipline. Since they spent most of their time training, when actually fighting they were usually the most determined warriors.

Anyone who infringed the rules could expect to be punished. Examples are offered in the Rule of the Templars. If the sin was slight, the knight might be ordered to recite the paternoster (the Lord's Prayer) a specific number of times, or he might be given some unsavory or unpopular task to undertake. On those occasions where the misdemeanor was more serious, the offending knight could be brought before the Chapter. His punishment would then be decided among his peers and there was no redress or appeal possible.

In the most extreme situations, a Templar knight could be stripped of his mantle and expelled from the order. This was a punishment that anyone would have avoided at all costs, because it would have made the offender a social outcast. An expelled knight would be about as popular, within his own family and friends, as an unfrocked priest – and of course people generally were far more religious during this period. There were, however, circumstances under which a seriously offending knight could redeem himself by becoming a monk – usually a Cistercian. If the knight in question showed true contrition and avowed himself to a life of seclusion, it might be considered that the stain had been removed from his character.

▶ An extraordinary theory – given the militaristic nature of the Order of the Temple – is that the secret beliefs of the Templars centerd on the Feminine; that, in effect, they were Goddess-worshippers. The Templars dedicated themselves to the Virgin Mary (right). On entering the Order, a new knight took an oath to "God and the Lady St. Mary" (or variations such as "God and Our Lady" or "God and the Blessed Mary"). The words of the Templar absolution were, "I pray to God that he will pardon you your sins as he pardoned them to St. Mary Magdalene and the thief who was put on the cross." Bernard of Clairvaux himself, when he had drawn up the Templar Rule, had commended the Templars to "the obedience of Bethany, the castle of Mary and Martha." (Mary of Bethany is normally regarded as the same person as Mary Magdalene.)

The most serious offence for a Templar knight was to show cowardice or even hesitation in the face of the enemy. It was made plain to all Templars that death or victory were their only options. Although there was a well-used convention at the time of "ransoming" captured knights, even the Templars' enemies were made to understand that this would never be an option in the case of a Templar knight.

◀ The birth of Saint John The Baptist with his father, Zacharias, writing his name on a tablet (from the Patzak Hymnal of 1335; ms. 1578, fol. 179). John the Baptist is the patron saint of the Knights Templar and the Knights Hospitaller.

▼ The young knight is being invested into the Knights Templar by the Preceptor, who has given him the Sword of John the Baptist.

Templars could never retreat unless outnumbered at least three to one and even much greater odds were not unknown. Templars were well trained, never showed any fear of the enemy or of death, and were special patrons of the Virgin Mary, whose name they would cry as they went into battle. This adoration for the Virgin Mary was something they had inherited from their patrons, the Cistercians, whose abbeys were usually named for the Virgin, who was Bernard of Clairvaux's personal patroness. They also showed special reverence for John the Baptist. Why this should have been the case is something of a mystery. It could conceivably have been because John the Baptist spent much of his time living in the desert, in self-imposed poverty of the sort that the Templars espoused.

7
Bankers, builders and tax collectors

TEMPLAR WEALTH AND ACQUISITIONS

Within a short time, hundreds of armed Templar knights were making their way to the Holy Land. Because the records of the Knights Templar, themselves, were lost in the capture of Cyprus by the Turks in the sixteenth century, we have no way of knowing exactly how many Templar personnel there were at any time. However, they became so common a feature and are mentioned so regularly in documents related to Western Europe and the Near East that there must at times have been many thousands. These first willing volunteers were put at the disposal of Baldwin II, King of Jerusalem, and the leaders of other regions where support against Muslim incursions was always welcome. From the outset the Templars fought with courage and distinction, mainly at first in skirmishes but, as time went by, in greater numbers, as in the battles of Montgisard and Ascalon in 1177, when over 500 Templar knights are known to have been present. During this stage of their history, the Templars totally fulfilled the expectations their own leaders and the Church had of them.

But their presence in the Holy Land was simply the beginning of the story. Soon the Templars began to build their own preceptories in the Near East, some of which eventually became sturdy castles. In order to transport personnel and equipment back and forth, the Templars also began to construct a sizeable and well-armed naval force, which would be used for commercial purposes as well as military ones. Their ships were kept in many different ports but the headquarters of the Templar Navy was at La Rochelle, France. The Templars had their own shipyards at La Rochelle but they would eventually need many different sorts of ships for differing tasks and sea conditions. It is likely that some of the Templar galleys were built in the Near East and in other locations in the West where the Templars held port facilities, for example, at Bristol in England.

Learning from the Cistercians, and possibly (though this is not confirmed) from a tremendously important, though now generally forgotten, monastic order known as the Tironensians, the Templars also excelled in building. The Tironensians, like the Cistercians, were a reformed Benedictine order created slightly after the Cistercians in 1105 and they became famous in their own day for their acumen in building.

As well as elegant churches, virtually impregnable castles and thousands of more humble farm buildings, the Templars created port facilities in France, England, Scotland, on the Mediterranean and in the Balkans, as well as on the coast of the Near East. They also almost certainly contributed to some of the most magnificent cathedrals ever to grace Western Europe – for example, that of Chartres in France.

The Templars were also soon building in other ways, which proved to be just as durable as methods using quarried stone. They began to supply promissory notes to pilgrims and merchants, to offer other banking services and to make profit as a result of their many transactions. They shipped pilgrims to the Holy Land and to other sites of pilgrimage (for a fee), and also moved luxury goods across the Mediterranean from the ports of the Near East to those of France and even Britain. Templars acquired land in strategic coastal areas in order to create their own harbor facilities and they were especially busy building and guarding toll roads.

The business opportunities were legion and the Templars never missed a possibility when it came to adding to the wealth of the Order. All this was undertaken on the pretext that equipping an army so far from Europe was prohibitively expensive but, within a few decades, their role as armed Christian knights became just one of their many enterprises.

La Rochelle was the Templars largest base on the Atlantic Ocean, and where they stationed their main fleet. From La Rochelle, they were able to act as intermediaries in trade between England and the Mediterranean. There is a legend that the Templars used the port of La Rochelle to flee with the fleet of 18 ships which had brought Jacques de Molayfrom Cyprus to La Rochelle. The fleet would have left laden with knights and treasures just before the issuance of the arrest warrant against the Order in October 1307, and the legend continues that the Templars would even have left for America, burying a treasure in Oak Island, Nova Scotia, Canada.

To the sea in ships

It is clear that from the start, the Templar Order wished to make itself as self-sufficient as the Cistercian Order from which it had sprung. We know this because they never subcontracted any of their needs to other organizations but organized their own farming, horse breeding, smithing, building and had specialists in all of their other requirements. To this end, one of the first needs was to construct and crew a sizeable force of fighting and merchant ships. Piracy was rife and particularly so in the Mediterranean. The Templars were constantly passing back and forth to the Near East, and so required formidable armed power at sea as well as on land.

In addition to sturdy ships, this meant that the Templar Order required its own harbor facilities for the shipment of personnel and equipment, and also quite soon for commercial enterprises. For example, what was the point in returning empty ships from the Near East when they could be loaded with potentially profitable cargo that could be sold back in Europe? And if there was extra space on outgoing and incoming vessels, why not offer safe passage to pilgrims, many of whom were traveling to exactly the same destinations as the Templars?

Eventually Templar ships plied the waters of the North Sea, around the coast of Britain, down the western seaboard of Europe, across the Mediterranean, the Aegean and even up into the Black Sea. Templar preceptories located at port facilities eventually became sizeable villages and ultimately towns. Examples are Bristol and Boston in England, and La Rochelle in France. In these locations, Templars could manage their own cargoes but also derive income from property rental, shipment charges and tolls of various sorts.

▼ A Templar Man-o'-War. Whilst in the early Crusades most knights and armies marched across Europe, it soon became clear that travel was faster by ship. However transporting the Templar army was no easy task and the Templar fleet was considered the largest fleet ever conceived. Once transported to the Holy Land they needed supplies. In all, each Crusade needed no less than 2,400 ships plying back and forth from European ports. The Templar fleet was distinguishable by a big red cross on the whitened sails. However, although there was generally a Templar onboard, the ships were "Chartered."

Templar captains must have made themselves into the best mariners of their day, because Templar ships were eventually sailing in Atlantic waters, all across the Mediterranean, up into the Balkans, the Baltic Sea and even the Black Sea. As we shall see, there is a persistent rumor that the Templar ships also crossed the Atlantic, visiting both North and South America. According to some accounts they were present in Nova Scotia and it has been argued that at least part of their wealth came from silver mines in South America. Perhaps these rumors can be taken with a pinch of salt, but even if these stories are not true, it cannot be doubted that Templar acumen in the skills of navigation funded many of the voyages of discovery that would follow in the next few centuries. Perhaps the most famous voyage of them all, that of Christopher Columbus to the New World in 1492, owed everything to Templar seamanship and knowledge that had been acquired across two extremely busy centuries. Columbus received many of his navigational maps from his father-in-law, Bartolomeo Perestrello, a noble, originally from Lombardy in Italy but who had come to Portugal and worked for Prince Henry the Navigator (who lived from 1394 to 1460). Prince Henry was the son of King John I of Portugal; he was Grand Master of the Knights of Christ, which was simply the Knights Templar under another name, who continued to exist in Portugal after their supposed destruction in 1307. Henry the Navigator had sent expeditions to all parts of the known world in his day and had a huge library of oceanic charts, many of which must surely have been of Templar origin.

▼ A monument to Prince Henry the Navigator (1394–1460) and the Portuguese Age of Discovery, Lisbon. Henry was the third child of King John I of Portugal. He was responsible for the early development of European exploration and maritime trade with other continents.

Banking

Travel of any sort in the twelfth century was fraught with difficulties. Road and sea connections were tenuous and dangerous, and there was always the possibility of being robbed. The rule of law in open and unguarded areas was in its infancy and pirates haunted every inlet and seaway, waiting to divest travelers of their gold and, most likely, their lives.

Templars were very successful at protecting pilgrims and merchants who were in their care, but they could not be with travelers all the time. This led to an ingenious solution that did more than anything else to create an important part of the world we now take for granted. Any pilgrim or merchant who wished to do so could lodge an amount of money at their local Templar preceptory. In return they would be given a promissory note that could be exchanged for whatever amount was owing to them from a Templar preceptory at their destination.

For example, a merchant could lodge a certain amount of money in London and collect his cash, in the local currency, from the Templar preceptory in Jerusalem. The promissory note the traveler carried was written in a code and the traveler would be given the answer to a question that would also guarantee only he could redeem his money. Such a traveler might draw from his original deposit at one or more Templar establishments during his journey, and his promissory note would be amended at each stage. This meant that nobody had to carry large amounts of gold around and so people were less likely to be robbed.

To charge interest, known as "usury," was not allowed in Christianity at the time, but the Templars got around this problem by making a profit from the exchange rate between one currency and another. Eventually, they became

▼ Eleventh-century fresco from a Cistercian Abbey in Italy shows St. Nicholas appearing to shipwrecked pilgrims. The Templars became viewed by many pilgrims as being as protective as St. Nicholas himself.

so powerful and indispensable that by the early years of the thirteenth century they could charge interest on such transactions, especially on loans to merchants and nobles, with impunity. The presence of the Templars ultimately allowed for credit transactions and also helped to fund new projects and enterprises, such as later crusades and royal building projects. So important did Templar money become in the open market that they eventually held entire kingdoms in their hands as collateral for the vast amounts kings had borrowed from them. This was almost certainly the case with the English King John (king from 1199–1216), was definitely so with Philip IV of France (king from 1285–1314) and was the main reason why Philip moved to destroy the Templars in 1307.

Another example of the reliance monarchs in Western Europe eventually placed on the Templars was the part they would come to play in the very administration of realms. For example, King John of England came to blows with the barons of England in 1215. He was ultimately forced to sign a document known as the Magna Carta, which for the first time defined the rights of citizens within his domains, as well as itemizing the limits of royal power. Not only was Aymeric, Master of the Templars in England, present when the Magna Carta was signed, he had been paramount in "persuading" King John that it was necessary. In all probability he did so because John owed so much to the Templars that it would not have been in their interests to see him overthrown.

▼ The Magna Carta is an English charter, originally issued in the year 1215 and reissued later in the thirteenth century in modified versions. The charter first passed into law in 1225. The Magna Carta was the first document forced onto an English King by a group of his subjects in an attempt to limit his powers by law and protect their privileges.

A sure foundation

In addition to their rapid growth as a banking institution, the Templars made themselves into expert builders. First and foremost they required stout fortresses in the Holy Land, which could act as preceptories for the Templar brothers but which would also be a suitable deterrent against Muslim attack. Once again, it appears that they fell back on their Champagne origins in the search for their acumen as builders and engineers. Bernard of Tiron, the founder of the Tironensian monastic order, was prevailed upon by Count Theobald VI of Blois, Troyes, Champagne and Chartres to create a college of architecture at Chartres. The Tironensians had been created as a breakaway Benedictine monastic order in 1105 and from the very start they dedicated themselves to improving existing building techniques, thus adding to the reservoir of architectural knowledge available in the West. At the Chartres college, the skill of the Tironensians was passed on. It is likely that the Templars were heavily represented at the college, originally as students, and that it was from here that their skill in building began to develop.

The Templars went on to create a string of almost totally impregnable fortresses. From Roche Guillaume, near Antioch in the north, down to Tiron des Chevaliers, near Jerusalem in the south, the huge walls of the Templar castles looked out on to the arid hills and valleys of the Holy Land.

There were also eventually significant numbers of Templar castles in Western Europe, and especially in France. These include Domme, in the Dordogne valley, La Couvertoirade, on the Larzac plateau,

▼ Chartres Cathedral was built in 1228 CE above an ancient geophysical portal. The financing and building of Chartres, involving the Knights Templar, is shrouded in mystery, which involves how the Templars found the knowledge, as early as the twelfth century CE, to build such a magnificent structure. The Knights Templar returned to France in 1128 CE, after ten years of study in Jerusalem, and began construction of Chartres, the archetypal Gothic cathedral and the World Soul in stone.

and La Cavalerie, in the Midi-Pyrénées. Templar fortresses were the last word in security and modernity in their day, and the later castles favored by Western monarchs were, in part, based upon the revolutionary techniques pioneered by the Templars. These included massive towers and keeps, specific areas known as "death traps," to confuse attackers, and a maze of internal passages that would see attackers becoming quickly disorientated and therefore more easily overcome, for example, areas accessible from above, so that arrows could be shot down onto the intruders or boiling water or oil poured upon them. Other death traps were areas just inside the inner gates of castles, where hidden recesses could be used to place unseen archers or knights to attack those entering the gate.

▼ La Couvertoirade, a medieval village of the Knights Templar. The castle of La Couvertoirade was built by the Knights Templar in the twelfth century, but the ramparts are the work of the Knights Hospitallers in the fifteenth century.

Templar churches and cathedrals

▼ The Church of the Holy Sepulchre, also called the Church of the Resurrection by Eastern Christians, is a church within the walled Old City of Jerusalem. The church has been an important Christian pilgrimage destination since at least the fourth century, as the purported site of the resurrection of Jesus. The First Crusade was envisioned as an armed pilgrimage, and no crusader could consider his journey complete unless he had prayed as a pilgrim at the Holy Sepulchre.

Building stout fortresses was of supreme importance to a fighting order such as the Templars but they were, first and foremost, monks. Despite their formidable reputation as warriors, the Templars spent a great deal of their time attending to the usual religious obligations of all monks. This meant that all Templar preceptories, castles and commanderies were built around a church. Many Templar churches were extremely beautiful and demonstrated the Templars' growing confidence in new architectural techniques. Most were, in some way, based upon the specific church building that was most revered by the Templar Order – the Church of the Holy Sepulchre in Jerusalem, which was a rounded church of the Eastern sort. This church supposedly marked the spot where Jesus Christ was laid in a tomb after his crucifixion and was therefore where the resurrection was said to have taken place. The Church of the Holy Sepulchre was originally built in the fourth century but had been significantly enlarged and altered in the following centuries.

A good example of the Templars' special reverence for the Church of the Holy Sepulchre is to be found at the Templar commandery and English headquarters in London. The Templar Church on the site still survives and its floor plan shows remarkable similarities to the floor plan of the Church of the Holy Sepulchre in Jerusalem.

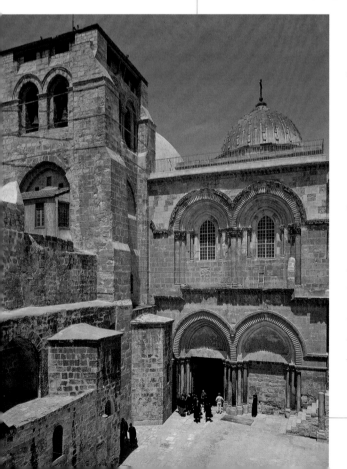

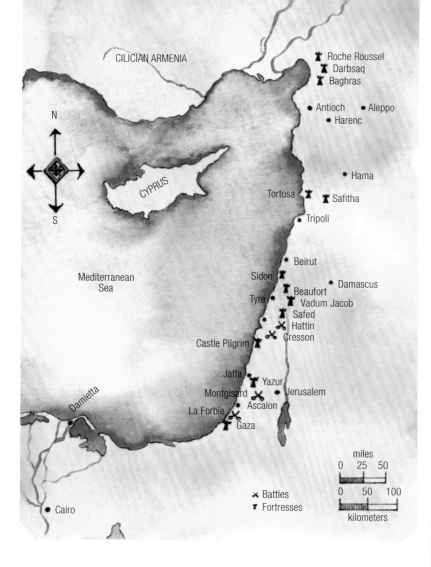

CILICIAN ARMENIA

Roche Roussel
Darbsaq
Baghras

N

Antioch • Aleppo
• Harenc

CYPRUS

• Hama

Tortosa Safitha

• Tripoli

S

Mediterranean
Sea

• Beirut
Sidon
Beaufort • Damascus
Tyre • Vadum Jacob
Safed
Hattin
Castle Pilgrim Cresson

Jaffa
Yazur
Montgisard • Jerusalem
La Forbie Ascalon
Gaza

Damietta

• Cairo

✗ Battles
Fortresses

miles
0   25   50

0   50   100
kilometers

◀ The Holy Land during the
Crusader period, showing Templar
fortresses and the location of
significant battles.

Sepulcher had a bearing on the design of Templar churches far from the
Middle East, though it is not correct to say, as some commentators have
done, that Templars always built round churches or churches with round
towers. Neither is it accurate to suggest that all rounded churches or
churches with round towers built in Western Europe were created by the
Templars.

Elsewhere the Templars did build many round churches, or more orthodox
buildings, though with round towers. Once again this was a reflection
of Eastern church-building techniques. The Templars also showed a

▲ The Church of the Holy Sepulcher in Cambridge is usually called the Round Church and was built by the Knights Templar in 1130. It was meant to emulate the Church of the Holy Sepulcher in Jerusalem and is one of only four surviving round medieval churches in Britain. The small nave is encircled by large Norman pillars, though the conical roof was added in the nineteenth century.

fascination for eight-sided and five-sided structures. These related in part to the floor plans of Eastern churches such as the Church of the Holy Sepulcher. It has been repeatedly suggested that the Templar fascination for the octagon in particular betrays the esoteric knowledge of the Order and that within it can be recognized many of the "inner secrets" of the Templar Order. However, it also has to be recognized that octagons were popular in the architecture of the time, in places with no known Templar influence. It could simply be that the Templars were following practices that were common in their day and, despite the protestations of fairly modern writers to the contrary, there may have been nothing esoteric about their architectural practices.

At the same time as the Templar Order was beginning to flourish, a massive exercise in church-building was taking place across Western Europe. Among these buildings can be numbered some of the most impressive cathedrals ever created by the hand of man.

Sorting out fact from possible fiction in the case of the Templar Order has always been very difficult. For example, there are persistent rumors that the Templars had a direct hand in the planning and building of some of the most impressive cathedrals of their era. This is particularly true in the case of Chartres Cathedral in France. The main body of Chartres Cathedral as we see it today was completed in a very short period of time, between 1194 and 1220. Chartres is built in the "Gothic" style, which began to proliferate in Europe at the time.

Gothic architecture differs from the earlier Romanesque style in that it had thinner walls, higher ceilings, much larger windows and an almost total reliance on a form of rounded and pointed arch known as an "ogive." Gothic buildings relied upon external flying buttresses for their inherent

▲ One of the defining characteristics of Gothic architecture is the pointed or ogival arch. Arches of this type were used in the Near East in pre-Islamic as well as Islamic architecture before they were structurally employed in medieval architecture.

◀ Close-up of two flying buttresses at Bath Abbey, Bath. A flying buttress is a free-standing buttress attached to the main structure by an arch or a half-arch. Instead of the buttress being stuck to the side of the building, it would form an arch leading away from the building and so carry the weight of the roof away from the building and down to the ground. Because the walls would no longer be carrying the weight of the roof, architects could allow larger windows filled with stained glass, and cathedrals looked lighter and more heavenly.

▲ The north door of Chartres Cathedral in France, built in the thirteenth century. One of the Templar legends surrounding this cathedral is that the Templars helped to pay for its construction in order to hide the Ark of the Covenant inside.

strength, rather than massive foundations and walls. Architectural historians have suggested that at least part of the Gothic style of architecture came from the Middle East, where Muslim architecture had been seen by crusaders. Some of the Muslim techniques were brought back to Europe and copied in the new churches and cathedrals of the period.

In the case of Chartres, there is no direct proof that either Templar money or skill was involved in the construction of the twelfth-century cathedral. But there are carvings around the north door at Chartres that some have interpreted as representing the Knights Templar bringing the Ark of the Covenant back to France after locating it beneath the ruins of the Temple in Jerusalem. These carvings show soldiers and knights with a cart carrying what definitely looks like the biblical description of the Ark. It has been suggested that the Ark was, or is, stored somewhere within the cathedral, and that the Templar's desire for a safe and secret hiding place for this artifact explains where the money came from to build Chartres Cathedral and why it was completed so quickly. It has to be admitted that any evidence linking Chartres with either the Ark of the Covenant or indeed the Templars is circumstantial, because definitive proof simply does not exist.

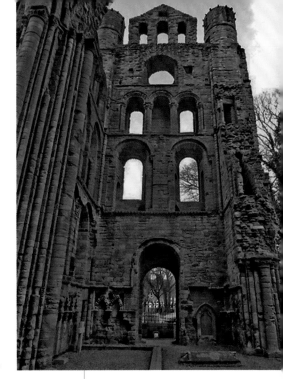

Perhaps we need not look too far to find a real and tangible connection between the Templars and the rise of Gothic architecture. The Templars were flourishing at exactly the same time Gothic architecture became so popular. They were also great builders in their own right. Being innovative, they used architectural techniques that were at the cutting edge of technology in their day. It is also possible that Templar skill in planning and building came from the school of architecture, set up in Chartres by Bernard of Tiron and the Count of Champagne. Whether or not the Knights Templar was instrumental in the running of this college is not known because knowledge of it, and indeed the Tironensians themselves, is not easy to find. Although the Tironensians at the height of their influence (by the end of the twelfth century) had 117 priories, mainly in France and Britain, they were integrated into other orders in the seventeenth century and, as far as researchers can tell, little information regarding the Order still exists.

▲ Kelso Abbey was once extremely wealthy, owning vast lands, churches, schools, farms and granges in the Cheviot Hills. It was built in 1128 by the Tironesian monks from France under King David I, and was dedicated to the Blessed Virgin of St. John in 1243. It boasted a superb library in medieval times and the Abbot of Kelso was granted the right to wear a mitre (liturgical headdress), which placed him at the top of the hierarchy of abbots in Scotland.

Not all trade in the twelfth century could take place by sea. There were large areas where merchants and travelers had no recourse but to rely on a generally poor road network in order to get from one place to another.

The Templars exploited this situation by building and repairing some of the most important trade routes, for example, those that led across the Alps from France into Italy. Once having taken on this responsibility, it seemed appropriate and even advantageous for the Templars to garrison such roads and provide armed soldiers to protect travelers from thieves and outlaws.

Such roads became toll roads and a charge was levied on anyone who wished to use the Templar routes. This proved to be another profitable source of income for the Templars in the decades that followed.

▲ Portrait of a medieval tax collector.

Tax collectors

As time went by, the Templars began to take on more and more responsibility for money passing back and forth across Western Europe and beyond. As we have seen, they became great bankers and lenders – even to kings and princes. Practically all the Plantagenet kings of England prior to 1307, and most of the French kings, were in their debt, but this was far from being the end of the Templars' acumen when it came to amassing greater wealth.

▶ Prince Richard I of Capua making a donation to the Abbey of St. Angelo in Formis, from a twelfth-century manuscript. This shows the regular practice of making donations to monasteries and churches during the Middle Ages.

It must have seemed a logical departure for kings, and then eventually popes, to use the Templars to collect taxes owed by the populace. Templars owned a great deal of land, much of which was rented out to tenants. They had become expert at collecting revenues on their own estates and, since they were so powerful, few people would argue with them. The finances of successive monarchs of both France and England were quite frequently run by the Templars, so it was in the interests of the Templars to assist kings in collecting revenue due to them. The Templars had all the necessary credentials, as well as being able to provide heavily armored escorts for gold being taken from one place to another. All of Western Christendom paid taxes to the pope, but this had been difficult to monitor or collect. Since the Templars had personnel and holdings in almost all places, and also because they were expert bookkeepers, all popes from the start of the thirteenth century relied on them to collect and pass on the papal revenues.

By the late twelfth century, in the later stages of their association with the popes, who received taxes from all parts of the Catholic world, the Templars found even more ways of earning income. All taxes owed to successive popes, and collected by the Templars, were held in their own hands until such time the funds were needed. This meant that vast amounts of gold were working for the Templar Order in the meantime. In earlier times this would have amounted to "usury," which was against canon law, but since the whole business was in the interest of popes, it quickly became overlooked. With such a mechanism in place, the Templars truly became bankers in the modern sense of the word. However, their position as tax collectors would eventually do little to endear them to the general public.

▲ Medieval tax collector's ivory seal.

▼ Examples of eleventh and twelfth-century coins. The gold augustalis on the left was produced by Frederick, Holy Roman Emperor and King of Sicily, Germany, Brindisi and Messina (1194–1250). The back of a gold Byzantine coin on the right, dated 1025, shows Jesus Christ.

8
Triumph and disaster in the Holy Land

THE COMING OF SALADIN AND THE CRUSADERS

SLOW RETREAT FROM THE MIDDLE EAST

From the very foundation of the Order, the Knights Templar fulfilled all their stated objectives as holy soldiers and as a result they were tremendously popular in the West. They had promised at the Council of Troyes in 1129 to be a holy Christian army, defending the faith in the Near East and, in fact, anywhere necessary – and this they had done. Their very existence, together with those of other military orders such as the Knight's Hospitaller, led to a new way of looking at armed knights and would help to create the whole notion of chivalry. Templar knights fought with great courage and tremendous discipline in some of the fiercest pitched battles that would take place in the Holy Land. For example, in 1177, when the forces of King Baldwin IV failed to stop Saladin (ca.1138–1193) and his army at Ramleh, and it looked as though Jerusalem might fall, a group of 500 Templars joined forces with Baldwin and, due to their almost fanatical assistance at the battle of Montgisard, Saladin was defeated so totally that he barely escaped with his life. Because of such exploits their very presence on the battlefield helped to spread fear and doubt among the enemy.

However, despite their presence, the survival of Christian domination in the Near East was a numbers game and one that the Templars could not address on their own. What the Holy Land required was massive commitment from the kings of Western and Eastern Europe, which was not forthcoming.

After the First Crusade, which had won Jerusalem and much of the Near East, further crusades followed, but on every occasion the commitment of the West was too little and often too late. At the same time Muslim resistance became greater as Islamic states in the region buried their own differences in order

◄ Nineteenth-century artist's impression of
Saladin, shrewd statesman and great commander
of the Muslims during the twelfth century

to combat the threat from Christianity. New Muslim rulers, especially Saladin, ruler of the Ayyubid Egyptians, began to appear who could inspire greater loyalty from the masses, thus creating formidable fighting armies that vastly outnumbered the Western presence in the Holy Land.

The result was a gradual erosion of Christian domination throughout the area. At first Jerusalem fell in 1187 and though it was very nearly recaptured by England's Richard the Lionheart in 1191, the reality of the situation was that Christians gradually held less and less territory in the Near East. They were driven back to the Mediterranean coast and, one by one, the towns and castles fell. Ultimately, the only city left to the Christians was Acre, and this fell to the Islamic forces in 1291. Even at this last stage of the defence of the Holy Lands the Templars fought like tigers, but to no avail.

Once the Holy Land was eventually lost altogether, in 1291, the Templars withdrew to positions within the Mediterranean, most especially to Cyprus which they held until 1307, and also returned many knights back to Western Europe. They remained an extremely potent fighting force, but their original intention had disappeared. They became useful scapegoats for the loss of the Holy Land, though in reality it was the crowned heads of Europe who had failed to commit themselves fully to defending the Holy Land. Nevertheless as the Templars lost popularity, the Order began to wane.

▷ Akko tower, Acre. Acre is best known as a Crusader's city, captured during the Third Crusade following which many of its walls and structures were built. Acre served as the headquarters for the Knights Templar and the Knights of St John Hospitaller. The Crusaders built walls around the city, controlled the shipping in and out of the port, and provided assistance to pilgrims throughout the Holy Land.

Muslims. In these battles there were many thousands of combatants on each side, while the Templars could probably only field a few dozen knights.

Better fortunes attended the battle of Ascalon, a city on the Mediterranean coast. There, in 1153, the Templars assisted in inflicting one of the most important defeats the Muslims would suffer following the abortive Second Crusade. In 1152, King Baldwin III of Jerusalem had repulsed a Turkish attack on his kingdom during which the Templars had fought with great determination. Spurred on by the success, Baldwin had rebuilt the ruined city of Gaza and had given it to the Templars to hold. It is not known how many Templars defended Gaza but they held it until 1244. Baldwin III then attacked and besieged the port of Ascalon, where the Templars made an almost suicidal charge on the city walls. Over forty Templars were killed, including the Grand Master, Bernard de Tremelay. But the Christians eventually prevailed, in no small part thanks to the Templar knights.

◀ Depiction of the Battle of Ascalon, 1099, between the Crusaders and the Muslims. Baldwin II siezed Ascalon in 1153.

The Battle of Montgisard

By 1177 the Muslim forces were under the command of a great general named Saladin. With his huge armies, Saladin threatened to overrun the Christians in the Near East altogether, but it was in one of the pitched battles fought against Saladin that the Templars really built their legend.

As a small contingency, with only 500 knights and their entourages, the Knights Templar had assisted in repulsing Saladin's army of around 26,000 when they attacked Gaza. The Christian army then pursued Saladin and brought him to battle at Montgisard, near Ramleh. There, under their Grand Master, Odo de St Amand, the Templars fought with unparalleled tenacity against vastly superior forces. What followed was probably the greatest victory since the capture of Jerusalem. The crusaders had succeeded in catching the forces of Saladin unawares, mainly because his army was spread over a large area and proved difficult to control. The Christians were able to impose such a crushing defeat on the huge Muslim army that many people declared the victory to be a miracle. The Templars had played a major role in both the defence of Gaza and the battle of Montgisard because, although there were very few of them, everyone at the time declared how fiercely they had fought and what an inspiration they had been. For a while they became the stuff of legend.

▼ 'The Battle of Montgisard, 1177', a painting by Charles Philippe Larivière. At the Battle of Montgisard, the Kingdom of Jerusalem, established by the First Crusade and led by Baldwin IV, defeated the renowned Kurdish military general Saladin. Learning of Saladin's plans to invade from Egypt, Baldwin's forces surprised his army en route and were triumphant despite inferior numbers.

▼ Map showing the routes of the Second Crusade (1145–1149). The armies of the French and German kings marched across Europe separately and were delayed by the Byzantine Emperor at Constantinople. The Germans were defeated by the Turks at Dorylaeum, and Conrad fled back to Nicaea, remaining there until the French arrived. Louis and Conrad and their diminished armies reached Jerusalem and in 1148 participated in a misguided attack on Damascus.

Templar knights were famous for their "squadron charges" in which a relatively small band of knights would thrust themselves into the midst of the enemy like a sharp spear. The tactic was used time and again to great effect, but in the end it was sheer force of numbers that overwhelmed the Christians in the Near East. Even the Templars, with their famous patee (spreading out at the extremities) red cross on their white mantles, could not alter the inevitable outcome.

A notable defeat suffered by the Templars came on 1 May 1187, when a small force of Templars, together with a few Knights Hospitaller and royal knights, fought the famous Saladin at the Battle of Cresson, near Nazareth. The Templars, under their Grand Master, Gerard de Ridefort,

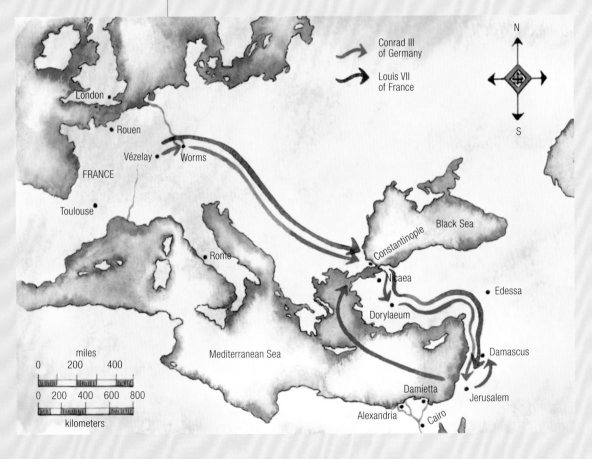

commanding only around 140 Templar knights in total, met an army of 7,000. With no thought of retreat, Gerard spurred his men into action. Almost all the Templars were killed, though Gerard himself managed to escape.

However, the greatest tragedy came a little later, in July 1187, when a pitched battle was fought near Tiberius, close to the Sea of Galilee. There, in a place called the Horns of Hattin, a Christian army under the command of the new King of Jerusalem, Guy de Lusignan, fought an army under Saladin that was ten times its size.

▼ Saladin and Guy of Lusignan after the Battle of Hattin. The Battle of Hattin (also known as "The Horns of Hattin" because of a nearby extinct volcano of the same name) took place on 4 July 1187, between the Crusader Kingdom of Jerusalem and the forces of the Ayyubid dynasty. The Muslim armies under Saladin captured or killed the vast majority of the Crusader forces, removing their capability to wage war.

▲ Statue of Saladin in Damascus. Saladin is a prominent figure in Kurdish, Arab, and Muslim culture. His chivalrous behavior was noted by Christian chroniclers, and despite being the nemesis of the Crusaders, he won the respect of many of them, including Richard the Lionheart. Rather than becoming a hated figure in Europe, he became a celebrated example of the principles of chivalry.

The crusaders, including a contingency of Templars, had been tricked by Saladin into marching from the Springs of Saffuriya towards Tiberius. Saladin had split his forces and set up diversionary tactics in order to mislead the crusaders. They made little progress and were constantly harried by Saladin's huge force. By 4 July 1187, the Christians found themselves in full armor, in the blazing heat without water and being taunted by the Muslims. They were completely surrounded and Saladin had brush fires lit to pour smoke on the crusaders and make their torment worse. The resulting battle was short but bloody and all the Knights Templar and Knights Hospitaller present, though having fought like demons, were either killed or captured.

◀ Crusader Knight Raynald beheaded by Saladin. Raynald of Châtillon, a Crusader Knight who took part in the Second Crusade and became famous because of his attacks on Muslim caravans. In 1187, at the Battle of Hattin, Raynald as well as King Guy and other Crusader leaders were captured by the Muslims. It is said that Saladin ordered Raynald to come into his tent and offered him life if he became Muslim. The Knight refused and was then beheaded by Saladin himself or one of his guards.

Of the Templars who fell into captivity, only the Grand Master, Gerard de Ridefort, was spared; all the others were summarily executed. Also put to death was the infamous Reynald de Châtillon, who was hated by the Templars and whose cruelty towards the Muslims had partly led to Saladin's popularity. Reynald de Châtillon was both treacherous and sly by nature, and could rarely be trusted, even by his allies. The Knights Templar were in no way responsible for the disaster but, despite their unquestioned valor in battle, it was from this time on that accusations of cowardice were made against them, both by leaders in the West and ultimately by the populace of Western countries, probably partly because their Grand Master survived.

▼ Raynald of Châtillon tortures Patriarch Aimery of Antioch. (From ms of William of Tyre's Historia and Old French Continuation, painted in Acre, thirteenth century).

The loss of Jerusalem

After the battle of Hattin, Saladin and his army began to capture numerous cities and towns, including Toron, Jaffa, Sidon and Beirut. By September the Muslims were at the gates of Jerusalem, a city swollen by thousands of Christians escaping the approaching armies of Saladin. Frantic negotiations took place between Balian of Ibelin, who was the highest-ranking noble in Jerusalem, and Saladin. Eventually, a suitable ransom was agreed upon and on 2 October 1187 the keys to the city were handed over and the citizens marched out in three columns, the first of which was led by the remaining few Templar knights.

The crusaders were eventually forced back to a smaller and smaller area and predominantly to the stronghold of Acre, a city in western Galilee, from where a third crusade was launched. For a while it looked as though ferocious fighters such as Richard I of England (the Lionheart) might win back Jerusalem. Richard was an honorary Templar and an inspired leader, but once again there were simply not enough Christian soldiers to combat the huge Muslim armies successfully.

The city of Safed, also in Galilee, was besieged in 1264 and during the battle ninety Templars were killed. Another eighty were captured, but they refused to convert to Islam and so were summarily executed.

▼ The Battle of Hattin, from a fifteenth-century manuscript. As a direct result of the battle, Islamic forces once again became the eminent military power in the Holy Land, re-conquering Jerusalem and several other Crusader-held cities. These Christian defeats prompted the Third Crusade, which began two years after the Battle of Hattin.

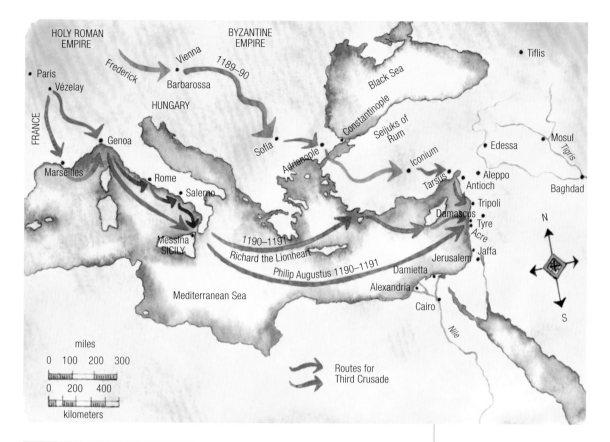

HOLY ROMAN
EMPIRE

BYZANTINE
EMPIRE

Paris

Vézelay

Frederick

Vienna

Barbarossa

1189–90

Black Sea

Tiflis

FRANCE

HUNGARY

Constantinople

Seljuks of
Rum

Mosul

Genoa

Sofia

Tigris

Marseilles

Rome

Adrianople

Iconium

Edessa

Salerno

Tarsus

Aleppo

Antioch

Baghdad

Tripoli

Messina
SICILY

1190–1191

Damascus

Tyre

N

Acre

Richard the Lionheart

Jaffa

Philip Augustus 1190–1191

Damietta

Jerusalem

Alexandria

S

Mediterranean Sea

Cairo

Nile

miles

0 100 200 300

0 200 400

kilometers

Routes for
Third Crusade

▲ Route of the Third Crusade
(1127–93). In 1189, Emperor
Frederick left Europe but drowned in
Anatolia a year later. In July 1190,
Philip of France and Richard of
England left for the Holy Land. By
July 1191, Acre was surrended to
the Crusaders, and Philip returned
to France soon after. In 1191,
Richard met Saladin at the Battle of
Arsur, and in 1192 he returned to
England.

◄ Richard I of England
(1157–99). He was known as
Richard the Lionheart, even before
his accession, because of his
reputation as a great military leader
and warrior.

The fall of Acre

▼ The Fall of Acre in 1291 depicted as if the crusaders were prevailing, which was not the case. The Siege of Acre (also called the Fall of Acre) resulted in the loss of the Crusader-controlled city of Acre to the Muslims. It is considered one of the most important battles of the time period. Although the crusading movement continued for several more centuries, the capture of the city marked the end of further crusades to the Levant. When Acre fell, the Crusaders lost their last major stronghold of the Crusader Kingdom of Jerusalem.

The city of Tripoli, in modern-day Lebanon, fell to Sultan Kalaun in 1289 and now all that remained for the Christian enclaves were a few unconnected strongholds, including the port city of Acre and a few crusader forts. Those who knew the situation best, including Guillaume de Beaujeu, current Grand Master of the Knights Templar, were aware that further resistance would only lead to more unnecessary bloodshed. De Beaujeu repeatedly tried to achieve favorable terms for a surrender of Acre, but for his pains it is suggested that he was labeled a coward and the Templars were accused, by both secular leaders and also some members of the Church, of trying to protect their financial interests in the Near East.

When all the negotiations were over, it was the Templars who remained steadfast in their resolve to protect the citizens of Acre, and they remained after practically all other available Christian forces had left by ship. Guillaume de Beaujeu was killed during the siege in April 1291 and, once the city itself capitulated, the remaining Templars fell back to their fortress on the edge of Acre. There they managed to hold out until 18 May, but they were finally defeated after a courageous last stand. Although some non-combatants and civilians escaped by ship, the whole Templar garrison eventually fought to its death.

The Templars' sacrifice at Acre was forgotten, but their desire to end the siege peacefully was not. Soon every trace of the once Christian-dominated Near East was wiped out for good and the West, stung by the disaster, looked around for people to blame. It was from this point on that the Templars began to meet with derision and even hatred among ordinary people. This would make it far easier for the whole Order to be attacked by an avaricious French king, Philip IV. Despite their rising unpopularity, estimates place the number of Templar personnel killed in the Near East, across the whole crusading era, as something like 20,000.

▲ Homage of Edward I (kneeling) to Philip IV (seated). As Duke of Aquitaine, Edward was a vassal to the French king.

◄ First seal of Philip IV of France (1286).

Troubles at home

Many of the Templars who escaped from the Holy Land found initial sanctuary in Cyprus, an island they had previously acquired from King Richard I of England. There they established new bases, while continuing to run their vast empire of trading and banking enterprises. Although the Holy Land was now closed to them, they still had many holdings in Western Europe. However, they were extremely unlucky during the closing years of the thirteenth century, not just on account of the disaster in the Near East, but also because of situations quite beyond their control that were taking place back in France.

▼ Twin Churches in Famagusta, North Cyprus. The larger of the two churches, built in the fourteenth century, belonged to the Knights Templars. When the last Grand Master and their other leaders were burned as heretics in 1313, the Order came to an end and the church was left over to the Knights Hospitallers who owned the adjoining building.

Although the official Templar headquarters was in Paris, the Order continued to have an essential base in Troyes, Champagne, where the whole adventure had begun. There they remained strong and were protected by the counts. As a region, Champagne had often been a thorn in the side of the French kingdom. It had a strong, integrated, aristocratic hierarchy that was invariably loyal to the wishes of the counts of Champagne, and it was strong enough on many occasions to stand against

◀ Joan I was the daughter of king Henry I of Navarre. Born in 1273, upon the death of her father the following year (1274) she became Countess of Champagne and Queen regent of Navarre. At the age of 13, Joan married the future Philip IV of France, becoming queen of France a year later.

▼ Seal of Joan I, Queen of Navarre; Countess of Champagne.

the wishes of successive French kings. Throughout the era of the Templars, it continued to be run as a more-or-less independent kingdom, despite the fact that the counts of Champagne owed allegiance to the French Crown.

The last independent ruler of Champagne was Joan of Navarre, the only surviving child of King Henry I of Navarre, who was also Count of Champagne. Henry died in 1274, leaving his daughter very much at the mercy of various crowned heads of Europe, all of whom looked longingly at Champagne and its wealth. Due to a series of blunders, mainly on the part of her mother, Joan found herself a virtual captive in Paris, where King Philip III had her betrothed to his son Philip.

▲ Engraving of Philip IV of France, who was determined to strengthen the French monarchy at any cost. He levied taxes on the French clergy of one half their annual incomes. This prompted Pope Boniface VIII to issue the bull *Clericis Laicos*, forbidding the transference of any church property to the French Crown.

▼ Bull of Pope Innocent III (1161–1216), which was similar to the Pope's letter of 1207 that condemned Templar pride. Innocent was a supporter of the Templare so it was particularly injurious when he critised them.

Born in 1268, Philip would inherit the throne of France as Philip IV in 1285. Joan became his wife, which meant that their son would eventually inherit his mother's lands, including Champagne. This might have been no problem were it not for the nature of Philip, who was secretive, scheming, cruel and despotic. Paradoxically, Philip gained the nickname of "*la Bel*," which means "the fair" or "the beautiful," though this was on account of his looks and not his personality.

Like all kings of France at the time, Philip inherited an impoverished nation. Regular crusades had drawn heavily on the French exchequer for decades, but the French Crown also met many difficulties relating to surrounding states and its need to enforce its rule constantly over them. Beyond this, Philip III's attacks on northern Spain, together with his own extensive crusading, had drained the exchequer dry. Since Philip IV wished to be an empire builder, he needed to get his hands on as much gold as possible. He extorted as much as he could from rich Jewish merchants and bankers, but it was not nearly enough to fund his many enterprises.

As a result, Philip turned his attention in the direction of one of the richest foundations in Western Europe – the Knights Templar. Almost everything played into his hands. Philip owed the Templars a vast amount in unpaid loans and they had even rescued him from an angry mob on more than one occasion at the start of the fourteenth century. Further to this, the Templars refused to make him an honorary member of the Order, as Richard I of England had been. Philip requested that this honor should be bestowed on him around 1304. Why he was refused is not specifically known, but his general unpopularity, his duplicity and his arrogance could all be contributing reasons.

Philip could not hope to move against the Templars whilst they fell under the direct protection of the Pope, but even here Philip had a plan. He arranged for the death of Pope Boniface VIII in 1303, at the hands of one of his court bullies, Guillaume de Nogaret, and Philip IV has also been condemned for the death of the next pope, Benedict XI, who was suspected to have been poisoned, again by Guillaume de Nogaret. Philip then took control of the cardinals, using a combination of bribery and bullying, and contrived to have one of his friends and allies raised to the papacy. That was Bertrand de Got, who, in 1305, became Pope Clement V. Clement was not allowed to reside in Rome, for fear that he might betray his old friend Philip – probably because Philip trusted nobody, not even his lifelong friends. Rather he was "encouraged" to set up his papal headquarters in Avignon, France.

▼ Pope Boniface VIII quarrelled with Philip IV and excommunicated him in 1301. Within days he was arrested by Philip's soldiers.

When Philip's son Louis (born in 1289) came of age in the early years of the fourteenth century, and with both Champagne and the Pope firmly in his hands, Philip was finally in a position to move against the Templar order.

9
Dark days

DESTRUCTION OF A HOLY ORDER

As far as Philip IV, King of France, was concerned, there were many reasons why the Knights Templar had outlived their usefulness. And although some other Western monarchs tried to find ways to protect the Templars, it must have been plain to most of them that the Templar order had become an anachronism – if not a downright danger. Nearly all monarchs owed money to the Templars, and many feared the presence of such a cohesive force without a real cause to follow.

It was being suggested throughout Europe that the Templars, now ejected from the Holy Land, were casting around to find a homeland of their own. This is probably incorrect but Philip IV almost certainly believed that the Templars were thinking of carving out a nation state for themselves in the south of France. The Templars already had a large number of castles and other properties to the south of the French region, especially around Carcassonne, and Philip would not have wanted them as his southern neighbor.

It was for this and a host of other reasons that Philip IV decided to destroy the order of the Knights Templar once and for all. He laid his plans amidst the greatest secrecy – or so it appeared. Nevertheless, as we shall see, it is almost certain that the Templars had at least some idea of what lay in store for them. From the last decade of the thirteenth century, the Templars knew that Champagne would eventually fall into French hands, and they were also more than aware of Philip IV's treacherous nature.

The Templars and Hospitallers were the closest of all the Orders. However, disputes between the Orders were renowned. Occasionally this rivalry broke out into open conflict and it was this negative side of their relationship that outsides focused on.

The Templars must also have watched the growing French interest in the papacy and could not have failed to appreciate that Clement V (Bertrand de Got) was a personal friend of King Philip. One of Clement's first actions was to suggest that the Knights Templar should merge with their old adversaries, the Knights of St. John (the Knights Hospitallers). This suggestion was rejected out of hand by the Grand Master of the Templars, Jacques de Molay, and, though for different reasons, Philip IV may well have agreed with him. Philip wanted the Templars destroyed, not amalgamated.

In 1306, Jacques de Molay was summoned to France by Pope Clement, to discuss the suggested merger with the Hospitallers. In September of 1307 Philip IV sent out instructions to his officials that the Templars would be arrested shortly and, on Friday 13 October 1307, every Templar property throughout the French domains was entered and all Templar personnel were arrested, including the Grand Master Jacques de Molay.

Fifteenth-century drawing of Pope Clement V, whose allegiance was with France rather than Rome. He was suspected by many outside France and England as a puppet of the King of France.

The accusations

Once the Templars had been arrested, Philip IV had to move quickly to consolidate his position. Jacques de Molay was horribly tortured and subjected to a string of almost unbelievable accusations regarding Templar conduct and true beliefs. The eventual charges were claimed to be as follows:

1. The Templars denied the Saints, the Virgin Mary and Jesus Christ as their Savior.

2. They were guilty of idolatry and especially the worship of a mysterious bearded head.

3. The Templars renounced the Holy Sacraments and they omitted specific parts of the Catholic Mass.

4. The Templar Grand Master and other Masters of the Order heard confessions, even though they were not ordained priests.

◀ "Jacques Molay prend Jérusalem 1299," 1846. Early 19th century painting by Claude Jacquand (1803–1878). During forced interrogation by royal agents in October 1307, Molay confessed that the Templar initiation ritual included "denying Christ and trampling on the Cross." He was also forced to write a letter asking every Templar to admit to these acts. Under pressure from Philip IV, Pope Clement V ordered the arrest of all the Templars throughout Christendom.

5. New recruits to the Order received obscene and unchristian kisses on their appointment – specifically on the mouth, navel, stomach, lower spine or buttocks.

6. The Order was obtaining funds illegally and also retaining money rather than using it for good purposes.

7. The Templars had kept secrets among their members on pain of death.

In short, the Templars were accused of many and varied forms of heresy and misconduct, all of which were punishable by death. Of course, many of the accusations were of the sort that would be hurled at any supposed heretic. Under great duress Jacques de Molay would only plead guilty to "denying Christ and trampling on the Cross" and he was forced to write a letter to all Templar personnel making it plain that they should all admit they had done likewise.

After the initial interrogation Jacques de Molay did everything in his power to have the charges against the Templars heard by a religious rather than secular court. On several occasions he retracted his original admissions, stating that they had been obtained under torture.

▼ This fourteenth-century illustration shows arrested Templars brought before Pope Clement V and King Philip IV where, once the threat of torture was lifted, they protested their innocence.

137

Templars on trial

Not long after the arrests, the Pope decreed that the Church itself should give judgment on the Templar Order, though other courts would be allowed to prosecute and punish individual Templars. Perhaps two hundred or so were brought to trial throughout France and some were condemned to death, mainly thanks to Philip IV's influence. In 1310 a total of fifty-four Templars were burned at the stake in and around Sens in France, and similar situations took place elsewhere within the French domains.

Other Western European monarchs watched and waited. It is said that Philip IV was furious that his fellow monarchs did not move against the Templars immediately in 1307. Edward II of England refused to do anything until he received a Papal Bull, thus giving those Templars at large in England the chance to escape or to prepare themselves for what lay ahead. The English Templars were not arrested until January 1308 and even then they were treated quite leniently. Almost no Templars were executed in England – most were eventually pardoned or else joined other monastic orders. In Scotland, no concerted action was brought against the Templars until 1309. By that time only two Templars could be found in the entire country.

▼ Illustration from a thirteenth-century manuscript of heretics burning theological books. Philip IV and Clement V accused the Templars of atheism, sodomy, blasphemy and more. In the Middle Ages, these accusations inspired suspicion and fear.

Templar fortunes differed greatly across mainland Europe and depended in part on any region's alliance to the French. In Spain, the Templars were originally arrested and some were tortured. However, in 1311, the Templars in most of Spain were judged to be innocent.

Italian Templars had plenty of time to flee the country because Templar trials there did not commence until 1309. Some Italian states found the Templars guilty and some exonerated them altogether. Only in Naples were all the Templars arrested and eventually executed.

▲ Illuminated letter ca.1350, showing a fool denying the existence of God. At the time it was accepted that no thinking person would renounce God, thus the Templars must be fools.

▼ The Templars, when not being tortured, maintained that they werre faithful Catholics and upheld the Rule that St. Bernard had given the Order in 1127.

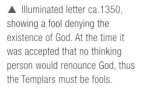

For reasons that are not entirely apparent, Portugal was less keen than any European state to move against the Templars. When it was eventually forced to do so by the Pope, all the Templars in Portugal were declared to be innocent. Even when the Order of the Templars was abolished by the Church, the Portuguese simply renamed it "The Knights of Christ" and everything carried on much as it had always done.

Perhaps the most bizarre situation was that which took place in Germany. In Mainz, on 11 May 1310, the Council of Mainz was sitting to discuss the matter of the Templars. The Council had been called as a result of the decrees of the Pope and was comprised mainly of local dignitaries. As they deliberated, into the chamber strode Hugo de Gumbach, Templar Master of Germany. He was followed by a large contingency of Templar knights, all in full armor. Hugo declared that he and his men were innocent of all charges and that they were quite willing to settle the matter by force of arms against any members of the Council who would stand against them. The Council quickly found the Templars of Germany innocent!

It was not until 1312, at the Council of Vienne, that the Order of the Poor Knights of Christ and the Temple of Solomon was finally dissolved by papal decree. It was ordered that all lands and property belonging to the Templars should henceforth pass to the Knights of St. John, though in reality very little Templar property found its way to the Hospitallers. In France, much passed to the Crown, as indeed was the case elsewhere because nearly all Kings benefited in terms of new lands as a result of the Templar's demise. In many cases, and especially where the Templars were never persecuted, they were still occupying the land decades later.

Jacques de Molay, the last Grand Master of the Templar Order, retracted his original admission of guilt when he discovered that he and his fellow masters were to be imprisoned for life. Philip IV flew into a rage as de Molay stood before him, together with Geoffroi de Charney, the Master of Normandy. Molay declared that the Templars had been guilty of no crime and that he would rather die than restate an admission that had been procured under torture. Both men were taken to a small island in the Seine, close to Notre Dame Cathedral in Paris, and on 18 March 1314 they were slowly roasted to death over a charcoal fire.

St.rangely enough the Pope had already found the Templars innocent of any heresy. In 2007, at the 700th anniversary of the Templar trials, the Catholic Church released a book detailing a parchment that was discovered in the Vatican library in 2001 (see the Epilogue for more on this). It is a detail of the Templar trials and clearly shows that the Pope intended to drop all charges against the Order. Doubtless Philip IV had other ideas.

▲ Philip IV attending the execution of Jacques de Molay and Geoffrey de Charney on 18 March 1314.

◄ Jacques de Molay and Geoffrey de Charney sentenced to the stake in 1314, from the chronicle of France, written by the monks of St. Denis.

▲ Philip IV the Fair inherited his father's debts, which he calculated would take over 300 years to repay. At the same time, his war with England had to be paid for.

▼ There are various legends concerning treasures that the Templars managed to hide from King Philip and that were later lost.

In search of Templar gold

Part of the reason why Philip IV had moved against the Templars was because of the debt he owed them. Philip had borrowed heavily from the Templars and the debt gave the Templars a moral right to "interfere" in the way France was run.

Obviously if the Templars ceased to exist, the debt would be wiped out at a stroke, but things went further in Philip's mind. Both as a prince and as King, Philip had often visited the Templar headquarters in Paris. The building was beautifully built and richly decorated. It contained fine works of art and was opulent in the extreme. It served to emphasize just how wealthy the Templar Order was. Philip also knew well of the Templar's many business ventures and particularly of their banking exploits.

At a time when one's liquid wealth, for example, gold and silver, was more than numbers on a bank statement, everyone kept their valuables locked in stout chests. Even kings had vast, well-guarded treasuries and Philip assumed that the same would be true in the case of the Templars.

The Templar commandery in Paris was one of the first places entered by Philip's soldiers on 13 October 1307, but the King must have been furious to discover that no treasure of any sort was to be found there. The same turned out to be the case all across France. Only a small proportion of the expected Templar personnel were arrested, because many of those who had been known to be present earlier were now missing, and despite the terrible torture that was meted out, no Templar gold was forthcoming in France.

There are two possible explanations as to why Philip found no sizeable treasury in any of the Templar properties he seized. While there is no doubt that the Templar Order as a whole was fabulously wealthy by 1307, Philip IV may have singularly failed to understand how the Order worked. The Templar Order was like a modern international company, with all manner of different enterprises spread across a vast area. It is quite likely that the majority of the Templar wealth did not exist in precious metals. Rather it was being put to work in order to earn more money. If this was the case, Philip could never have located the main Templar treasury, because it simply did not exist in the way he envisaged.

This explanation only partly answers the puzzle regarding Templar gold, which to some extent must have existed, because the Templars ran a large banking operation from all their commanderies. This would have been especially true in Paris and other large French towns and cities. However, it was not simply the gold and many of the Templar personnel that had gone missing. Down on the west coast of France the main Templar fleet in Western Europe was moored in La Rochelle. Historically, this was the Templars' most significant port and, since returning from the Holy Land, it is generally suggested that until the fateful day, La Rochelle was filled with the Order's ships.

▲ Templar commandery in the village of Chanonat (Puy-de-Dôme, France). The commandery was the smallest division of the European landed estate or manor under the control of a commander or of an order of knights. Originally, commandries only existed for the Order of Knights of St. John of Jerusalem. Commandries of the Knights Templars were known as preceptor and preceptory.

▼ Chapel of the Knights Templar Commandery at Élancourt (Yvelines, France).

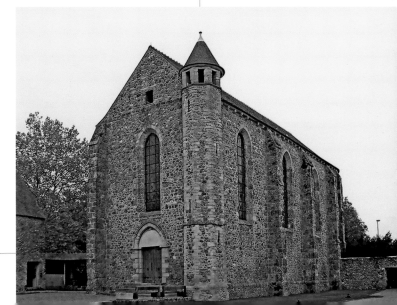

▶ Nineteenth-century drawing of *The Knight's March*, a poem by Alfred Lord Tennyson which perpetuated the romantic and idealised myths about medieval knights such as the Knights Templar.

When the French king's soldiers arrived at La Rochelle on the morning of 13 October 1307, they must have been stunned to find all the ships missing. The fleet had sailed during the night, which must stand as proof positive that the Templars knew exactly what Philip IV was planning and had decided to make certain the fleet would not be captured. It therefore has to be considered a possibility that the Templar gold had been transferred to the fleet and that the Templar treasure went wherever the ships had gone.

This explanation fails to address the situation of Jacques de Molay, because some would think it almost certain that if the Grand Master knew what was about to happen, he would have left France before Philip could act. A counterview suggests that if the Grand Master had betrayed any sign that he was aware of the French king's intentions, he might have actually forced the authorities to act earlier than they did. In other words, it is at least a possibility that Jacques de Molay knew only too well that he would be arrested, but that his commitment towards his brother knights and the Order as a whole outweighed any consideration for his own safety. Jacques de Molay spent months playing for time while in captivity, constantly admitting his guilt and then retracting the admission. By doing so, was he simply offering more time for the Templars in France and elsewhere to escape or to assume new identities?

▼ The Templar fleet left La Rochelle days before King Philip IV arrested the Templars across France. It has been said that the fleet transported the Order's treasure to various locations around the world.

10
Templar mysteries

ENDURING LEGENDS OF A HOLY ORDER

The continuing interest in the Order of the Knights Templar springs in part from the mystery surrounding what their "true" beliefs and practices may have been, especially i the charges brought against them had any substance, and the many puzzles associated with the pivotal period around the beginning of the fourteenth century. Philip IV and his tame pope had good reasons for wanting to destroy the Templars, but is it possible that they were in any way guilty of the long list of crimes against Christianity that were brought against them in 1307?

Were the Templars a genuinely heretical sect and what was the significance of the strange bearded head they were said to worship? Why had the Templars so often refused to fight in the crusade fought against the equally mysterious Cathar of southern France between 1209 and 1229? At the time the Templars stated that it was their remit to fight against Saracens, by which they almost certainly meant Muslims, but their attitude to the Albigensian Crusade made Pope Innocent III furious. He is supposed to have called them "unchristian" and even "necromancers." Did the Templars have beliefs that were broadly similar to the Cathar, and is this why they were so reluctant to become involved?

There is also a continued debate about the disappearance of the Templar fleet on the night of 12 October 1307. Those commenting at the time and since were adamant that there was a significant fleet at La Rochelle. Where could so many ships have gone without being detected by one or more of the European powers whose own seaways surrounded those of western France? Was the missing Templar gold loaded upon these ships prior to the Templar arrests and, if so, where did it go and to what purpose was it put in the following decades?

All manner of suggestions have been made regarding the Templar fleet. Some commentators assert it sailed directly to Scotland and they bolster the theory by pointing to the possibility that Templar knights fought for the Scots against the English in the great Scots victory at Bannockburn in 1314. To counter this, other researchers have pointed out that many of the ships the Templars used in the Mediterranean, and which would have been moored at La Rochelle, would have been quite unsuitable for use in the North Sea. Popular legend also suggests that the Templar fleet made its way to Spain, Portugal or even the Americas, though proof for any of these possible destinations is scant. It seems that everyone has their own theory but the orthodox annals of history simply declare that the Poor Knights of Christ and the Temple of Solomon effectively ceased to exist after 1307.

Bearing in mind that the attacks made on the Templars in countries outside of France came late, were half-hearted and in some places non-existent, is it likely that such a large and complex organization as the Templars would simply disappear? Despite the Templar dependence on Champagne and France, is there any place to where they could have moved their center of operations from which they could continue to exert a powerful influence on the developing financial and political development of Europe?

▷ The Battle of Bannockburn on 24 June 1314 when Edward II was defeated by King Robert the Bruce. It was a significant Scottish victory in the Wars of Scottish Independence.

Guilty as charged?

At his last public audience in 1307 the Templar Grand Master, Jacques de Molay, retracted any confession he had previously made under duress. He declared the Templars to be innocent of all charges and demanded both Philip IV and Pope Clement V to join him for judgment before God himself. Developing fascination for the Templars was almost immediately fostered in the knowledge that both Philip and the Pope died within a year. In all probability this was simply a coincidence, but even present-day supporters of the Templars might cry "divine intervention."

There is no doubt that during most of the two centuries of their official existence, the Templars had literally been a law unto themselves. They overturned the Christian laws on usury, sometimes failed to fight, even when their supposed head, the Pope, demanded that they should; they undoubtedly held negotiations with some Muslim leaders that would have run contrary to the wishes of those in charge of the Christian Near East. They also kept some of their inner activities and practices secret. Nobody had dared to interfere with their order and successive popes had been happy to leave the Templars to their own devices, as long as the taxes were rolling in. It does seem highly likely that such a secretive order, made up entirely of men, began to deviate somewhat from Catholic orthodoxy. Between the cloistered repression of a monastic life and the testosterone-fuelled frenzy of bloody battle lay what must have been one of the most unnatural societies imaginable.

It is surely not unlikely that in such a homogeneous and potentially homosexual society as that represented by the Templars, rites and practices specific to the Order itself began to develop. Ritual kissing is a good example. Nobody at the time would ever have admitted to homosexuality, except perhaps under extreme torture, because it was punishable by death, but some Templars, when interrogated (including the Grand Master,

▼ An engraving of Jacques de Molay. According to one story, he opened his shirt when he met Clement V a month after his arrest, in order to display the marks of torture on his body.

Jacques de Molay), did admit to the ritual kiss. Templar knights were also monks and so were supposed to absent themselves from any sort of sexual congress. In all probability most of them did, but it would have been strange indeed if there had not been significant exceptions.

Many of the accusations made against the Templars were quite general and could easily have been invented by Philip and his henchmen. However, this does not explain the accusations of spitting or trampling on the Cross, which seems very specific and quite unusual. Perhaps there is some truth in it, because in one of the trials in France, a young Templar recruit told of how he had been in possession of a crucifix. When it had been seen by one of the older brothers the young man had been told: "Don't have too much faith in this – it is too young!" Of course, the young Templar's admission was made under duress, but he could have been telling the truth. Can we infer from this that the Templars had become committed to some other religion, for example, some form of Judaism, which of course predates Christianity by many centuries? Nevertheless, they fought ferociously for the Christian cause and it is entirely possible that all the accusations of heresy were false.

▼ The execution of King Louis XVI of France in January 1793. Some believe that the the disposal of the French monarchy was the final retribution of Jacques de Molay and the Knights Templar.

The bearded head

Perhaps some light might be thrown on true Templar beliefs in the knowledge of one particular accusation that was made against them. It was suggested that the Templars had a special reverence for a mysterious bearded head, which it was said the Templars called "Baphomet." This came out at the Templar trials that were held across France and became a familiar, if somewhat strange, accusation against the Templars. However, no example of such an icon in relation to the Templars seems to have been produced.

Whole books have been based on the conception of Baphomet and what it might have represented. But there could be a simple explanation. The Templars had a great regard for the prophet John the Baptist, whose feast day they held in special reverence. The biblical description of John the Baptist makes it plain that he lived wild and unkempt in the desert, so he is always depicted in art as having long hair and a beard. John the Baptist was eventually beheaded on the orders of King Herod Antipas and his severed head was presented on a plate to the beautiful temptress Salome. During a period in which credulity regarding supposed religious relics reached incredible proportions, it is not unlikely that the Templars believed they had acquired all or part of the head of John the Baptist. Such supposed relics are known to have existed. The Cathedral at Amiens in France claims to have the remains of John the Baptist's face that was brought to France from Constantinople.

The theory could also be borne out by a legend that is still circulating in the northern English town of Halifax, where the Templars once owned land. The parish church in Halifax is dedicated to St. John the Baptist and it

▼ "The Beheading of St. John the Baptist," 1640, a painting by Carel Fabritius (1622–1654).

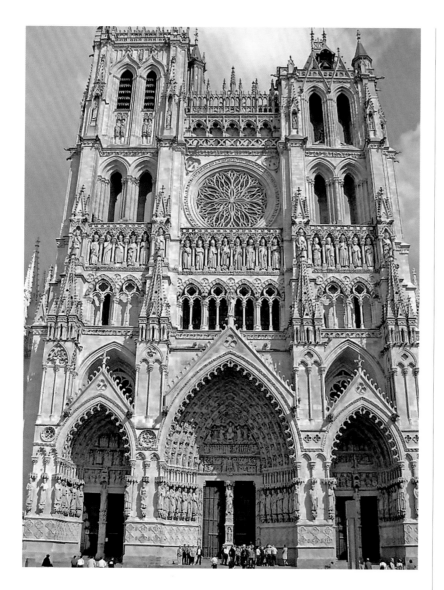

◀ The Cathedral of Our Lady of Amiens or simply Amiens Cathedral is the tallest Gothic church and largest cathedral in France. In 1206, Amiens became one of the most important pilgrimage destinations in Europe when the head of St. John the Baptist was brought back from Constantinople by Crusaders. This impressive relic would be the principal source of revenue for the cathedral for years to come, enabling the construction of the grand Gothic cathedral that endures today.

▼ Piece Hall Gate Coat of Arms, Halifax, West Yorkshire.

has been suggested, though probably wrongly, that the name "Halifax" derives from the words "Holy Face." The coat of arms of Halifax carries a gory representation of the severed head of John the Baptist to this day. Legends in the town make reference to a relic of John the Baptist once kept by the Templars and other parts of the same relic could have been held in other Templar commanderies.

▶ Salome presenting the head of John the Baptist to Herodias. A woodcut by Albrecht Dürer (1471–1528).

However, there is no direct evidence that the Templars actually claimed to have the head of John the Baptist. Like so much else regarding the Order, we have to rely on legend and hearsay. Praying to saints for intercession was common during the Templar period and so Baphomet could have been nothing more than a specially revered patron saint to the Templar Order.

Despite this explanation, the story of Baphomet was complicated when the eminent English-born biblical scholar and expert in ancient biblical texts and ciphers, Hugh Schonfield (1901–1988), declared that the name Baphomet might be part of a cipher, known as the "Atbash code." The Atbash code was Jewish in origin and was a simple word substitution code used regularly in the composition of the Dead Sea Scrolls. Schonfield had noticed that when the name Baphomet was broken down by the code it became "Sophia," which is not only the Greek word for "wisdom," but also has strong feminine religious connotations. This has caused some modern researchers, such as myself and the Canadian Templar expert St.ephen Dafoe, to suggest that the Templar reverence for the Virgin Mary may have been a cover for an entirely alternative and somewhat pagan version of Christianity focusing on "the Great Goddess" of many ancient religions, and that the bearded head was itself a sort of pictographic code for something radically different. This may seem unlikely in view of the Templars' apparent commitment to the Christian cause, but the suggestion is that they, together with many of the aristocrats of Champagne, were involved in a Christian "schism," rather than celebrating an entirely different religion.

Because the name "Baphomet" bears a slight resemblance to the name Muhammad, some commentators have wondered whether the Templars had become influenced by Islam during their long stay in the Holy Land. This is perhaps the least likely explanation, because human representations of any sort are a complete taboo in Islam.

▲ Lévi's (1810–1875) Baphomet image employed in the later nineteenth century to suggest Baphomet worship by Freemasons. Baphomet, an imagined pagan deity, first appeared in the eleventh and twelfth centuries but was later used as a term for a pagan idol in trial transcripts of the Inquisition of the Knights Templar in the early fourteeenth century.

▲ The cross at Montségur.

The Templars and the Cathar

Although the matter was not included in the accusations, the Templars had come under suspicion as early as the thirteenth century because of their refusal to become involved in a war fought by the Catholic Church in the south of France. This is generally known as the Albigensian Crusade and was directed at a community known as the Cathar. As we have seen, even when the Pope at the time, Innocent III (Pope from 1198 until 1216) ordered the Templars to take part, they simply refused to do so. Their unwillingness to be involved must surely have led people, including the Pope, to believe that the Templars had some sympathy with the Cathar version of Christianity, which was considered by the Roman Catholic Church to be a heresy.

▶ Montségur in southwestern France is famous for its fort and was one of the last strongholds of the Cathars. The present fortress on the site, though described as one of the "Cathar castles," is actually of a later period.

The Cathar were a large community who thought of themselves as being Christians, but their basic doctrines differed markedly from those of the Catholic Church. They held that there was a good creator God, but that he had an evil counterpart in the physical world. Cathars were mostly vegetarian, lived fairly blameless lives, accepted that men and women were equal and had a generally more liberal view of sexuality than orthodox Catholics of their period. The Cathar did not maintain great churches or cathedrals and did not have an established priesthood. Their communities were split into two sections: those who lived normal everyday lives similar to their Catholic neighbors and an inner community of ascetic, almost monastic, men and women known as Parfaits and Parfaites.

▶ This French picture ca.1415 shows the expulsion of the "Albigensians" from Carcassone in 1209. The first crusades were against Christians who had separated from the Catholic Church in Europe.

▼ The Battle of Muret during the Albigensian Crusade in 1213. Simon de Montfort was the leader of this crusade (1209–29), which aimed to destroy the Cathars under Raymond of Toulouse.

The Catholic Church could not accept such a radical departure from its own doctrines and authority in its midst. In 1209, a twenty-year campaign was launched against the Cathar states, during which the Cathar were all but eradicated from Europe. During the whole of the Albigensian Crusade, the Templars showed themselves to be reluctant to become involved. In some battles they absolutely refused to take part.

There could be a series of quite understandable reasons for the Templar attitude to the Cathar. There were many Templar castles and commanderies in the region of Languedoc, where the Cathar were most active. The Templars had maintained good relations with the Cathar and some, for example, the fourth Templar Grand Master, Bertrand

◀ Pope Innocent III (1198–1216), arguably the most powerful pope in history. He was a vigorous opponent of heresy and proclaimed a crusade against the Albigensians (Cathars).

▼ A twentieth-century illuminated manuscript from Languedoc, showing the capture of Montségur Castle, where over 200 Cathars were burned alive during the Albigensian Crusade. In March 1244, 10,000 French Catholic troops set fire to the castle, turning the Cathar defenders into a human bonfire.

de Blanchefort, came from Cathar families. Even many orthodox Catholics at the time maintained that the Cathar were no threat and that they lived blameless lives; it is also known that the Templars believed their fight to be against Muslims in the East.

The Templars' reluctance to involve their Order in the Albigensian Crusade drew attention to them at the time. Some researchers and some writers – for example, Baigent, Leigh and Lincoln – have claimed that the core beliefs of the Templars may well have been closer to those of the Cathar than the orthodox Catholic Church.

▲ Seal of Robert the Bruce, King of Scots.

▼ A statue of Robert the Bruce, King of Scots, at the Bannockburn memorial.

The missing Templar fleet

In the opinion of most modern researchers, who are also in possession of knowledge regarding the political situation regarding the Templars at the beginning of the fourteenth century, many of the accusations brought against the Templars in 1307 were patently absurd and there is surely no mystery about them at all. Whether some of them were true or not, in the main they were created in order to justify Philip's intended destruction of the Order. Nevertheless, there are puzzles regarding the events of 1307 that do require further attention. First amongst these must be the disappearance of the Templar fleet, which sailed out of the pages of history on 12 October 1307.

Could the Templar fleet have sailed to Scotland? At the time, Scotland was at odds with its southern neighbor England and was ruled by King Robert the Bruce. Bruce had been excommunicated from the Catholic Church as early as 1306 for murdering a rival, so at the time of the attacks made on the Templars he was not, strictly speaking, a Roman Catholic. He was also being sorely pressed by the English and needed all the military help he could obtain. Although it is far from proven, it is an often-held Scottish Nationalist belief that Templar knights who fled to Scotland after 1307 fought with Robert the Bruce against the English in the decisive battle of Bannockburn in 1314. The battle was a crushing defeat for the English and bought Bruce valuable breathing space.

◄ Numerous templar tombstones from Argyll can be seen in the Kilmartin graveyard. They prove that the Order of the Temple survived in Scotland after 1312, the year in which it was officially dissolved.

▼ The Kilmartin St.ones are a collection of 79 ancient graveslabs at Kilmartin parish church. The earliest stones date back to the thirteenth or fourteenth centuries, with the most recent ones dated 1707 and 1712. Originally, the stones would have been laid flat on the ground to cover a grave. After the Reformation, however, many of the stones were moved, and in 1956 they were moved inside a shelter to protect them from the weather. It has been suggested that several of the slabs may commemorate Knights Templar but this theory is unproven.

There are numbers of Templar-style graves to be found in parts of Scotland, especially in Kilmartin, Argyll, and attention has been brought to this area as a possible retreat for at least some Templars fleeing France. Whether these graves truly are those of Templar knights is a matter of conjecture. However, it is very unlikely that an entire fleet of Templar ships could have evaded the English on its way to Scotland in 1307 and there is no documentary evidence that the Templar presence in Scotland was significantly enlarged at this time.

An even less likely theory is that the Templar ships made their way across the Atlantic to the shores of North or South America. The idea that Templar ships had already visited the New World by 1307 cannot be dismissed out of hand. The Templars were well represented in Bristol, England, where they had their own port facilities, and even fishermen from

▶ Temple Church, Bristol, a 1899 postcard by Harvey Barton. The church was built in the twelfth century by the Knights Templar. It was rebuilt in the late fourteenth century and underwent substantial restoration work in the late nineteenth/early twentieth centuries.

Temple Church, Bristol.   Harvey Barton

▼ A painting of Christopher Columbus by Alejo Fernández (1475–1545) between 1505 and 1536.

Bristol appear to have been quite familiar with the vast lands that lay to the east. They regularly sailed to the Grand Banks of Canada to catch cod. The existence of America appears to have been common knowledge long before the expeditions of either Christopher Columbus (1492) or John Cabot (1497). There is a well-known legend suggesting that Henry St. Clair, Earl of Orkney, had been there in the late fourteenth century and also Viking sagas about visits to the land beyond Greenland that could only have been North America.

The idea of a full-scale escape to the Americas by the Templars in 1307 is not tenable for a number of reasons. Many of the ships that disappeared from La Rochelle were not of the type that could have successfully negotiated the Atlantic Ocean. But

probably the best proof against the idea is that although isolated European buildings, encampments and possible staging posts from an early age have been found down the eastern seaboard of the United St.ates – for example, the Newport Tower in Rhode Island and L'Anse aux Meadows in Newfoundland – there is no evidence that large-scale emigration from Europe ever took place at this very early date.

The most probable explanation for the missing Templar fleet is that some or all of the missing ships traveled to Portugal. The journey would not have been a protracted one and Portugal never persecuted the Templars. Rather, as already mentioned, it simply renamed the Order "The Knights of Christ." Portugal would hardly have crowed about an illegal and supposedly heretical force hauling up in its country, but common sense suggests it is the most likely explanation for the disappearance of the fleet.

▲ The Templar's Rotunda of the Convent of Christ in Tomar, Portugal; a stronghold built in 1160 by Gualdim Pais, the provincial Master there.

In the following centuries Portugal took a decisive lead in voyages of exploration, and for a while began to carve out a large empire for itself. It is entirely possible that the maritime prowess of the Portuguese was bolstered by the arrival of Templar ships and personnel in 1307. The Portuguese at the time would have been reluctant to let either Philip IV of France or the Pope know that the Templar fleet had found safe harbor in their country.

▼ The north side of the medieval Port of Trani. Just to the left of center is the church of Ognissanti. In the 1100s the church stood at the corner of the grounds of a large Knights Templar hospital, and was built as its chapel. Trani was a major embarkation and supply point for the crusades of the 1100s and 1200s.

The Swiss connection

A relatively recent theory regarding the destination of many of the French Templars and their gold may well hold the key to the mystery. To the east of France and protected by the high peaks of the Alps lies the nation state of Switzerland. In 1307 this region was ruled by the Holy Roman Empire, which had ruled the area for centuries. At this stage, what would eventually become Switzerland was represented by a series of disparate regions, allied only by the local people's hatred for their despotic rulers.

As early as 1291, three of the regions (cantons) of what would eventually become Switzerland, Uri, Schwyz and Unterwalden, began an uprizing against the Hapsburg Holy Roman Emperors that would span many decades. The most notable successes were at the battles of Morgarten in 1315 and Sempach in 1386, during which the Hapsburgs were soundly beaten. Quite soon other cantons began to join the new confederacy, and the state of Switzerland was born out of common interest.

▼ The Battle of Morgarten , 15 November 1315, when a Swiss Confederation force of 1,500 infantry archers ambushed a group of Austrian soldiers of the Holy Roman Empire near the Morgarten Pass. The Swiss, led by Werner St.auffacher, defeated the Austrians, who were under the command of Duke Leopold I of Austria.

Many of the early events in Swiss history were played out during the same pivotal decades in which the Templars were attacked and destroyed in France. Bearing in mind what Switzerland eventually became, in terms of banking and especially regarding its almost fanatical secrecy, it is entirely possible that many of the French Templars, together with a great percentage of their vast wealth, never sailed from La Rochelle but rather melted quietly away into the

mountains over a period of months prior to October 1307. The inference here is that the Templars had plenty of warning of what was facing them in France, as seems likely.

Switzerland is remote, naturally protected by its mountains and, as the Hapsburgs discovered to their cost, almost impossible to attack with conventional forces. Surely nowhere within easy striking distance of France could have made a better bolthole for the Templars who, it must be remembered, were masters of the many trade routes that existed throughout the Alps. An escape to Swizerland and the use of Templar skills in fighting to protect the region and buy it autonomy would have been eminently sensible. Even the eventual flag of Switzerland offers a clue, because the Swiss white cross on a red field is simply a reversed version of the famous Templar red cross on a white field.

▶ The Retro Choir, Rosslyn Chapel. Rosslyn Chapel, properly named the Collegiate Chapel of St. Matthew, was founded on a small hill above Roslin Glen as a Roman Catholic collegiate church in the mid-fifteenth century. In later years the chapel has featured in speculative theories regarding Freemasonry and the Knights Templar although it was built 150 years after the dissolution of the Order. The chapel supposedly has many Templar symbols, such as the "Two riders on a single horse" that appear on the seal of the Knights Templar.

The Templars, Rosslyn Chapel and Freemasonry

St.anding in stark isolation, close to the modern village of Roslin, near to Edinburgh in Scotland, is the fabled Chapel of Rosslyn. This extremely ornate, small gothic structure was built in the middle of the fifteenth century by William St. Clair, who had formerly been the Earl of Orkney and who came from an illustrious, originally Norman family that had supported the Scottish Crown for three centuries.

Tradition asserts that Rosslyn Chapel is merely the "lady chapel" of what was originally meant to represent the eventual collegiate church of St. Matthew. However, not long after the part of Rosslyn Chapel that does exist was constructed, the forces of the Reformation swept across Scotland, putting paid to any thought of building new Catholic churches, which Rosslyn Chapel had been.

There is no doubt that Rosslyn Chapel is one of the most ornate churches in Britain, let alone Scotland, and it is a "confection in stone," replete with carvings inside and out. By the nineteenth century it had become a virtual ruin but a visit there by Queen Victoria, who loved the place, ensured that the fabric of the building was repaired and from the mid-nineteenth century on, Rosslyn Chapel became a normal parish church. But almost from the time it was first built, the chapel has been the repository of rumors, fables and traditions that ally it with both the Knights Templar and the much later Freemasons.

▼ The grave slab of William de St. Clair (1297–1330). He died in Spain fighting the Moors while taking the heart of the dead king, Robert the Bruce, on a crusade to Jerusalem.

▶ Interier of Rosslyn Chapel showing the Apprentice's Pillar. The pillar has become an iconic mystical symbol. There has been speculation that it is hollow and contains some treasure– the Holy Grail or maybe the mummified head of Christ.

▼ A carving said to support the Templar connection to Rosslyn Chapel – a knight in chain and carrying a lance shares his horse with another who barely hangs on at the back. The similarity to the Templar's seal of two riders on one horse is clear.

There is actually nothing to connect Rosslyn Chapel directly with the Knights Templar, except for a couple of small carvings that could conceivably be meant to represent Templar knights. It seems to have been during the nineteenth century that stories began to circulate which suggested that whatever the first Templar knights had discovered below the Temple of Solomon in Jerusalem had somehow found its way to the safety of Rosslyn and been buried in a series of supposed passages below the structure.

The authors Christopher Knight and Robert Lomas, with professional, architectural support, suggested that what remains of Rosslyn Chapel was never actually intended to be any bigger than it is. In their book, *The Hiram Key*, they suggest that Rosslyn Chapel is actually a copy of what people in the fifteenth century believed the Jerusalem Temple once looked like and that it was for this reason the structure was created by the St. Clair family, who, it was said though never proved, had a close connection with the Knights Templar.

Knight and Lomas further proposed that Rosslyn Chapel was not only a post- Templar construction, but that it was also the place where Templarism ultimately turned itself into Freemasonry.

Modern Freemasonry began in 1717, when a number of already existing Freemasonic Lodges in London joined together to form what is known as Grand Lodge. Prior to this, Freemasonry had existed in Scotland, with the oldest known lodge, that of Kilwinning, Scotland, claiming to date back to 1140. The history of Kilwinning Lodge associates its formation with the Tironensian abbey of Kilwinning, where, the traditions of the Lodge claim, local masons were trained within the abbey and regular chapter meetings began.

▲ A junior warden introduces a candidate to a Lodge for admission as an apprentice Freemason in the seventeenth century.

▶ Freemasons' Hall, London, has been the center of English freemasonry for 230 years. It is the headquarters of the United Grand Lodge of England, the oldest Grand Lodge in the world, and also the meeting place for over 1000 Masonic lodges. The building was completed in 1933.

Freemasonry these days has nothing to with stone cutting or carving in any real sense. It is a fraternal organization created for the moral and spiritual good of all men who wish to take part. Freemasons engage in somewhat strange ceremonies, filled with biblical allusions and pseudo-history, which elevate members through a series of stages, or degrees, all of which are designed to be uplifting and instructive. Knight and Lomas claim in *The Hiram Key* that Freemasonry actually came about in the fifteenth century and that it was the brainchild of William St. Clair, builder of Rosslyn Chapel, as a means of making sure that the chapel's secrets were kept safe. Even today Freemasons make a series of oaths, on pain of death, not to divulge anything regarding aspects of their ceremonies, secret words, symbols or secret handshakes.

The Hiram Key proved to be a bestselling book and Rosslyn Chapel was part of the remit of *The Holy Blood and the Holy Grail* by Baigent, Leigh and Lincoln, a book which also suggests that the building is associated with the transformation of Templarism into Freemasonry.

Several forms of Freemasonry throughout the world have degrees that are named after the Knights Templar and which claim to confer the rank of Templar Knight on participating members. In addition, there are now a number of known Masonic organizations named after or relating to the Knights Templar.

▼ The Freemasons' square-and-compasses symbol adorns a wall in Washington, D.C.'s Masonic House of the Temple. The square-and-compasses symbol has its roots in the craft of stonemasonry. Most of the trade's tools are represented somewhere in the symbols of the Freemasons. Masonic scholars explain that the square reminds Masons to ensure that their actions conform to a "square of virtue," while the compasses symbolize self-control over their passions.

Since the Knights Templar was a monastic order created and sanctioned by the Roman Catholic Church, which destroyed the order in 1307, none of the more recent Knights Templar, Freemasons or other organizations can be said to have any direct connection with their historical namesakes. Nevertheless, the name and reputation of the Knights Templar is probably more popular today than it has been since the foundation of the Order in the twelfth century. The Poor Knights of Christ and the Temple of Solomon have been fascinating people for over 800 years, a situation that is not likely to alter in the near future.

In a strange twist to the story of the Knights Templar, who in every real sense were outlawed and abandoned by the Catholic Church in 1307, a document has recently been found in the Vatican that shows the Templars were actually pardoned by Pope Clement V. Details of this extraordinary document can be found in the Epilogue.

▲ St. Clair Family Memorial, Rosslyn Chapel. Rosslyn Chapel has been in the ownership of the St. Clair family since its foundation in 1446. The tale of the Saint Claire (Sinclair) family has long provided a source of controversy and mystery for scholars, conspiracy theorists, and religious followers alike. Interest in the St. Claire family originates from Henry Sinclair (1345–1400), who was the direct descendant of William St. Claire, the first Grand Master Mason of the Grande Lodge of Scotland, a position that was subsequently held by other members of the St. Claire family. Linked to this, others say, is the fact that not only were the St. Claire family members of the Knights Templar and thus keepers of the Holy Grail – they were the Grail. That is to say, the St. Claire family actually descended from the Jesus family bloodline.

Epilogue

THE VATICAN'S ADMISSION

In 2001, an Italian academic and historian called Barbara Frale, from the University of Venice, was conducting research in the Vatican library when she came upon a document that had been incorrectly filed. This may turn out to be one of the major finds of the twenty-first century, especially as far as the Knights Templar is concerned.

The faded and stained document has become known as the Chinon Parchment, because it was compiled at the castle of Chinon, which is in Tours, France. It relates to an investigation into the accusations made against the Knights Templar in 1307 and in particular to the interrogation of a number of high-ranking Templar personnel, including Grand Master Jacques de Molay.

Those carrying out the investigation were doing so under the direct instruction of the Pope, Clement V. The representatives of the Pope included a number of high-ranking cardinals specifically tasked with getting to the bottom of the accusations the Templars faced after the attacks made on the Order by King Philip IV of France.

▼ Pope Nicholas V established the library in the Vatican in 1448. It is one of the oldest libraries in the world and contains one of the most significant collections of historical texts.

Under investigation were Jacques de Molay, Grand Master of the Templars, together with Hugo de Pérraud, preceptor of France, Geoffroy de Gonneville, preceptor of Aquitania and Poitou, Raymbaud de Caron, preceptor in the Outremer (the Holy Land) and Geoffroy de Charney, preceptor of Normandy. All the accused had previously been excommunicated by the Church in 1307 and each of them, in turn, was interrogated by the appointed cardinals. After a lengthy deliberation, all the Templar personnel present were found innocent of any serious crime and were brought back into the fold of the Church in 1308.

Some of the more famous among the charges initially made against the Templars in October 1307, such as heresy, incorrect forms of service and collusion with the enemy, were put to the accused by the examining cardinals. With a few minor exceptions, all were denied by the accused, and their testimony was accepted by the Pope's enquiry. Some slight doubt remained regarding a tacit acceptance of homosexual activity within the Order – but which for any large monastic institution would hardly be surprising. There was also some ambiguity regarding ritual kisses and, in particular, spitting on the Cross. In the case of the latter, it seems likely that the denial of the Cross at the time of a Templar's admittance to the Order may well have represented some sort of test, probably associated with possible capture by enemy forces in the Holy Land. As far as can be ascertained, the Templars during this investigation never admitted to defiling the Cross in any way.

▲ The execution of Jacques de Molay. During years of torture, Jacques de Molay refused to disclose the location of the funds of the Order and he refused to betray his comrades. On 18 March 1314, de Molay was tried by a special court. As evidence, the court depended on a forged confession, allegedly signed by de Molay. He disavowed the forged confession which, under the laws of the time, was punishable by death. Another knight, Guy of Auvergne, Preceptor of Normandy, likewise disavowed his confession and stood with Jacques DeMolay. King Philip ordered them both to be burned at the stake that day. They were taken to an island on the Siene and burned.

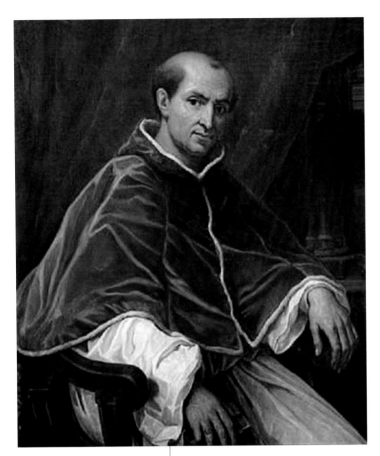

▲ Portrait of Pope Clement V, Avignon, France. Following the death of Benedict XI in 1304, he was elected Pope Clement V in June 1305. He is memorable in history for suppressing the order of the Knights Templar and executing some of its members.

Despite these slight aberrations from normal Catholic practice, the accused were reinstated to the faith without question and the commission declared the Templar Order to be innocent of the charges that had been laid against it. Unfortunately this made very little difference, because Pope Clement V was completely at the mercy of Philip IV, who had clearly decided from the outset that the Templars had to go. The implication is that when Jacques de Molay and Geoffroy de Charney went to their deaths in 1314, burned over a slow fire in Paris, they did so not as proven heretics but as true children of the Catholic Church.

Within a year of the deaths of Molay and de Charney, both the Pope and King Philip IV were themselves dead. The Templars were by this time dispersed and even if there had been the will to do it, the reconstruction of the Order as it had formerly existed was out of the question.

The Vatican agreed to create copies of the Chinon Parchment to coincide with the 700th anniversary of the destruction of the Templars, in 2007. Only 799 copies were created, forming part of an inordinately expensive book, most of which have found their way to libraries and universities. The book, entitled *Processus Contra Templarios*, became available on 25 October 2007.

The publication of the Chinon Parchment has been taken as an apology on behalf of the present Pope, Benedict XVI, for the fact that despite being found innocent, the Templars were treated so abysmally early in the fourteenth century. At least one modern Templar offshoot, "The Association of the Sovereign Order of the Temple of Christ," a Spanish organization, has announced that it intends to pursue a case for substantial financial damages against the Vatican through the Spanish courts. It claims that in the fourteenth century the Vatican seized property from the Templars with a modern value of €100bn.

▲ In 2007, the Vatican released a crucial document, not seen for 700 years, which restores the reputation of the Knights Templar whose leaders were burned as heretics when the order was dissolved in 1314, finding them to have been innocent of heresy. The Vatican has now published the entire documentation of the papal hearings, convened after King Philip IV of France arrested and tortured Templar leaders in 1307 on charges of heresy and immorality. It includes the Parchment of Chinon (above), the decision made by Clement in 1308 to save the Templars and their order. In it, Pope Clement V absolved the knights of heresy, but the order was still disbanded for "the good of the church" in 1312, under pressure from King Philip IV of France.

Whether or not such a legal wrangle could ever be decided upon after such a long period of time remains to be seen. What is not in doubt is that the Templars had been accused of purely religious crimes and so, having been found innocent by the highest ecclesiastical court available, the deaths of all those Templars who perished before and after the trial can be seen as political murders rather than legally sanctioned punishments.

▼ A late-Romantic depiction of a lone weary Templar Knight returning from the Crusades, by the German painter Karl Friedrich Lessing (1808–1880).

Glossary

Albigensian Crusade The name is taken from the city of Albi, in Languedoc France, which was the center of the Cathar movement. The crusade marked the beginning of the end for the Christian sect and was instigated by Pope Innocent III, leading to a twenty-year military crusade against the Cathars from 1209 to 1229 which saw their strongholds fall and their lands given over to those French noblemen who took part in the campaign.

Anti-popes Are those leaders within the Roman Catholic Church who reject the authority of the elected head as the Bishop of Rome and set up as rivals, usually with the backing of secular kingdoms or Cardinals. Between the third and fifteenth centuries it was not uncommon for anti-popes to challenge the pope sitting in Rome.

Ark of the Covenant A chest or strongbox said to have been constructed to hold the two stone tablets that bore the Ten Commandments, given by God to Moses that are the moral foundation for both Judaism and Christianity.

Babylonians The people of Babylon, a small town believed to have originated in the third millennium BC in what is present day Iraq.

Baphomet An idol which the Knights Templar were accused of worshipping. The name has come to be associated with an occult half-man half-goat figure from the late nineteenth century onwards.

Benedictines Those monks following the Rule of St. Benedict of Nursia, who founded the order in central Italy in the sixth century AD.

Bernard of Clairvaux Twelfth century AD French abbot and driving force behind the Cistercian order of monks. He was also deeply involved with the politics of the day, advising popes and Kings of France. In later life he was awarded Doctor of the Church, an honor given to those who have been of great importance or contributed to theology or doctrine.

Byzantium   Present day Istanbul, Turkey, this was originally an ancient Greek city that became known as Constantinople and was capital of the Greek speaking Roman empire for more than a thousand years. It was captured by the Ottoman Turks in 1453 and became part of the Ottoman empire.

Cathars   A dualist sect living mainly in southwest France, Provence and northern Italy during the eleventh to thirteenth centuries.

Christianity   A monotheistic religion based on the teachings of Jesus. Originally a small Jewish sect it spread across parts the Middle East to become the dominant religion within the Roman Empire by the fourth century AD. The largest groupings within Christianity are the Roman Catholic Church, the Eastern Orthodox Churches, which split in 1054.

Cistercians   A Catholic order of monks and nuns that rejected the wealth and privilege found within the church by the late eleventh century AD. They aimed to return to the original teachings of St. Benedict of Nursia through an emphasis on manual labor and self-sufficiency.

Council of Clermont   Called by Pope Urban II in 1095 AD the council, which included bishops, abbots and many prominent lords, discussed the problems facing the church at this time. A significant problem for Christian Europe was encroaching Muslim armies who were at the time besieging the city of Byzantium that had requested military assistance earlier the same year. At the end of the council Urban II called for the faithful to liberate the eastern churches and although he did not specifically say so his words were widely interpreted as a call for the re-taking of Jerusalem and the first Crusade.

Council of Troyes   Called by Pope Honorius II to deal with the disputes amongst the Bishops of Paris and local church matters the council's agenda became heavily influenced by Bernard of Clairvaux who used it to create the Knights Templar as the order of Poor Knights of Christ and the Temple of Solomon.

Crusades   Seven crusades were launched in total, across a period of over 150 years (1095 to 1250), with the intention of retaking Jerusalem as a Christian city. Knights from across Europe traveled and in many cases remained in the Middle East attempting to preserve as Christian not only the Holy city of Jerusalem but lands from Antioch to Tyre.

Dead Sea Scrolls   972 scrolls written in Aramaic, Greek and Hebrew and discovered at Khirbet Qumran between 1947 and 1956. The scrolls contain both biblical and non-biblical texts and appear to be the library of a Jewish sect that hid them in the caves to protect them from the advancing Roman army during, or prior to, the First Jewish Revolt, 66–70 AD.

Freemasonry   One of the oldest surviving secular brotherhoods in the world and although its origins are obscure it has been claimed that it dates back to the stonemasons who built the Temple of Solomon in Jerusalem, tenth century BC.

Gothic architecture   Known at the time as The French St.yle it was a form of architecture that flourished in the high and late medieval period, twelfth to sixteenth centuries. Its characteristics include pointed arches, ribbed vaults and flying buttresses that gave buildings a large interior height.

Grand Master   The title bestowed upon the head of many orders of knights, including the Knights Templar, Knights Hospitaller and the Teutonic Knights.

Holy Land   Originally a term taken from Judaism referring to the Kingdom of Israel it became widely used in Christian Europe and referred to the lands of religious significance associated with the teaching of Jesus, with Jerusalem as the most holy place.

Holy Sepulcher   Revered as the site where Jesus was buried it is now a church within the walled old city of Jerusalem, known to Western Christians as The Church of the Holy Sepulcher and Church of the Resurrection to Eastern Christians. It has been a place of Christian pilgrimage since the fourth century AD.

Hughes de Payen   A French knight born in the Champagne region. With Bernard of Clairvaux he co-founded the order of Knights Templar and became its first Grand Master. He died in Jerusalem in 1136 AD.

Islam   A monotheistic religion first practiced in Mecca, in what is now known as Saudi Arabia, in the seventh century AD. It is now the world's second largest religion. Most Muslims, the followers of Islam, belong to either the larger Sunni or Shia sect.

Jacques de Molay   The last Templar Grand Master who died in 1314 AD. Tortured and burned at the stake on the orders of King Philip IV of France.

Knights Hospitaller   The Order of Hospitallers were founded from a group of men attached to the Amalfitan hospital in Jerusalem in 1023 AD. Their duties were to protect and care for the poor, sick or injured pilgrims in the Holy Land. After the First Crusade the order became a religious and military group and continues to this day as the Sovereign Military Order of Malta, a Roman Catholic group promoting humanitarian causes.

Magna Carta   In 1215 the feudal Barons of England forced King John to agree to and sign a charter that limited his powers and preserved their privileges. This Great Charter was the precursor to a second charter 1297, The Great Charter of the Liberties of England, and of the Liberties of the Forest.

Middle East   This is a region that is generally taken to encompass Western Asia and North Africa.

Papal Bull   These are charters issued by the popes of the Roman Catholic Church. Originally the papal bull was used for all public pronouncements or communications but in recent centauries has tended to be used only for solemn religious decrees.

Peter the Hermit   Born in Amiens, France, in the mid-eleventh century AD, he became a monk and was present at the Council of Clermont when Pope Urban II called for the First Crusade. Peter traveled through France and Italy preaching and is thought to have help promote the Crusade as a cause. Peter was one of the leaders of the Peoples Crusade in 1096 and although this group did include some knights and other military personnel Peter's command was made up of paupers and was unarmed. Peter believed that God would look after and protect him and is followers but it was not to be and through starvation and attacks the majority of his pilgrims were dead by the time they reached Constantinople. Peter did struggle on and finally reached Jerusalem but, he soon returned to Europe where he established a monastery at Neufmoustier, in what is now Belgium.

Preceptories   These were generally a church and its living quarters for those various orders of monastic knights, such as the Knights Templar or Hospitaller. The preceptory would be governed by a Preceptor who was answerable only to the Grand Master.

Richard the Lionheart   King Richard I of England ruled from 1189 to 1199 AD although he rarely visited the country preferring to spend his time in his French lands, that included amongst others the duchies of Normandy, Aquitaine and Gascony. In 1187 Pope Gregory III called for the Third Crusade and along with Philip II of France and the Holy Roman Emperor Frederick I, Richard took part.

Robert of Molesme   A Christian saint he was born a nobleman in Champagne and entered the church aged 15. He rose to be an abbot of Saint Michel-de-Tonnerre in the reforming atmosphere of the time he left to form a new monastery in Molesme, Burgundy. As the new monastery's wealth grew and its piety and sanctity waned Robert again became disheartened and left to form a new order with some companions deep within the forest. The abbey they built was named Citeaux and led to the birth of the Cistercian order.

Rule of Conduct   Prior to the formation of the Knights Templar you could choose to devote your life to religion and become a monk or become a knight and devote your life to defending your country and lord. The rule of conduct was the document that framed the new order that created a wholly new entity of fighting monks who would go to war to defend their God.

Saladin   Salah-ad-Din Yusuf ibn Ayyub was a Kurdish Muslim born in Tikrit, in what is now know as Iraq, in the first half of the twelfth century AD. A brilliant soldier and military genius he was respected by many of his opponents and has become an almost mythical figure remembered for his principles and chivalry. The military defeats he inflicted upon the Crusaders signalled the end of Christian power in the Middle East.

St.ephen Harding   Born in Dorset, England, in the eleventh century he joined Sherborne Abbey as a boy and remained there into adulthood until be became a traveling scholar. Eventually moving to Molesme Abbey he first me Robert of Molesme and moved with him to start Citeaux Abbey. He served the abbey at Citeaux for 25 years and as leader of the Cistercian Order had a large impact on its formation and growth.

Temple Mount   A site in Jerusalem revered in the religions of Judaism, Christianity and Islam and as such one of the most contested religious sites in the world.

Temple of Solomon   This legendary First Temple, on Temple Mount, was said to have been built by the ancient Hebrews after he captured and occupied Jerusalem. According to the Hebrew Bible it was constructed by King Solomon in the tenth century BC and was designed to hold the Arc of the Covenant. The First Temple stood for over 400 years until it was destroyed by the armies of Nebuchadnezzer II in 587 BC.

Tironensian A Roman Catholic order of monks and nuns named after the main abbey in Tiron, France. It was founded in 1106 by the Benedictine monk Bernard d'Abbeville and came to be formed as a reaction to the laxity of the Benedictine order at the time and a return to a strict monastic life as taught by St. Benedict of Nursia. The order were famed as an order of master craftsmen and five years of its creation the order owned over a hundred priories and abbeys in western Europe.

Usury The medieval term for charging interest on a loan which was outlawed throughout this period.

Vatican library Currently housed in Rome this is the library of the Roman Catholic church and was established in 1475 although it is in fact much older and holds over 75,000 manuscripts and over a million books.

Bibliography

Baigent, Michael, Leigh Richard, Lincoln, Henry, *The Holy Blood and the Holy Grail*, London: Arrow Books, 1982

Baigent, Michael, Leigh Richard, *The Temple and the Lodge*, London: Jonathan Cape, 1989

Barber, Malcolm, *The Trial of the Templars*, Cambridge: Cambridge University Press, 1978

Barber, Malcolm, *The New Knighthood: A History of the Order of the Temple*, Cambridge: Cambridge University Press, 1994

Barber, Micahel, Bate, Keith, *The Templars: Selected Sources*, Manchester: Manchester University Press, 2002

Bernier, Fancine, *The Templars' Legacy in Montreal, the New Jerusalem*, Kincraig: Frontiers Sciences Foundation,2002

Burman, Edward, *Supremely Abominiable Crimes: The Trial of the Knights Templar,* London: Allison & Busby, 2002

Butler, Alan, Dafoe, St.ephen, *The Warriors and the Bankers*, Dorking:Templar Books, 1998

Butler, Alan, Dafoe, St.ephen, *The Templar Continuum*, Dorking:Templar Books, 1999

Knight, Christopher, Lomas, Robert, *The Second Messiah*, London: Random House, 1997

Laidler, Keith, *The Head of God: The Lost Treasure of the Templars*, London: Weidenfeld & Nicholson, 2002

Laidler, Keith, *The Divine Deception*, London: Headline, 2000

Markale, Jean, *The Templar Treasure at Gisors*, Rochester: Inner Traditions, 2003

Nicholson, Helen, *Templars, Hospitallers and Teutonic Knights: Images of the Military Orders*, Leicester: Leicester University Press, 1993

Nicholson, Helen, *The Knights Templar: A New History*, St.roud: Suttton Publishing, 2001

Partner, Peter, *The Murdered Magicians*, Oxford: Oxford University Press, 1981

Picknett, Lynn, Prince, Clive, *The Templar Revelation*, London: Bantam, 1997

Ralls, Karen, *The Templars and the Grail*, Wheaton: Quest Books, 2003

Read, Paul, Piers, *The Templars*, London: Weidenfeld & Nicholson, 1999

Seward, Desmond, *The Monks of War: The Military Religious Orders*, London: Penguin Books, 1992

Sinclair, Andrew, *The Sword and the Grail*, London: Century, 1993

Sinclair, Andrew, *The Secret Scroll*, London: Sinclair St.evenson, 2001

Upton-Ward, Judi, *The Rule of the Templars: The French Text of the Rule of the Orders of Knights Templar*, Woodbridge: Boydell Press, 1992

Index

Abreviamen de las Estorias 24
Acre 77, 123
  Akko Tower 117
  Fall of 126
Al-Aqsa Mosque 65
Albi, Languedoc 182
Albigensian Crusade 148, 156, 158, 182
Aleth 59
Alexius Comnenus 21
Al-Masjid al-Nabawi 20
Almery of Antioch 123
Amalfitan Hospital, Jerusalem 55
Amalric I 44
Amiens 186
  Cathedral 153
anti-popes 182
Aquitaine 177, 186
  Duke of 127
Arabian Peninsula 20
Arabs 122
Aragon 85
Aramaic 184
Ark of the Covenant 46, 110, 182
Arsur, Battle of 125
Ascalon 98, 118
  Battle of 118
Atlantic Ocean 99, 101
Auch, France 46
Avignon, France 131, 178
Aymeric 103
Ayyubid dynasty 117, 121

Babylonians 48, 182
Baigent, Michael 159, 172, 189
Balantrodoch 89
Baldwin I, King of Jerusalem 26
Baldwin II 26, 47, 68, 72, 98
Baldwin III 44, 118
Baldwin IV 116, 119
Baldwin of Boulogne 26
Baldwin of Rethel 26

Balkans 99, 101
Baltic Sea 7, 33
Bannockburn, Battle of 148, 149, 160
Baphomet 152, 155, 182
Barber, Malcolm 189
Bar-sur-Aube 35
Bate, Keith 189
Bath Abbey, Bath 109
Bauernfeind, Gustave 44
Bayeux 22
Beirut 124
Belgium 30, 38
Benedict XI 131
  Rule of 71
Benedictines 18, 39, 58, 62, 104, 182
Bernard of Clairvaux 32, 51, 55, 60, 62–3, 68, 70, 74, 90–1, 94, 182, 185
Bernard of Tiron 111
Bernier, Francine 189
Bisol, Geoffroi 45
Black Sea 7, 101
Books of Hours 37
Boston, England 100
Bristol 98, 100, 161
Burgundy 30
Butler, Alan 189
Byzantine Empire 14, 183

Cabot, John 162
caliphs 20
Canada 99
Carcassonne 134, 158
Castille 85
Castillo de los Templarios 10
Catalonia 38
Cathar 148, 157, 183
Champagne 9, 30, 33, 35, 149
  Count of 36, 57, 63, 111
  Countess of 129
  Fairs 51, 64
Chanonat 143
Chartres 99, 111
  Cathedral 48, 104, 109

Zodiac Window 49
Cheviot Hills 111
China 33
Chinon 176
  Parchment 178–9
choir monks 61
Christian Knights 99
Christianity 6, 15
  Eastern 14
Church of the Holy Sepulcher 106
Church of the Resurrection 106
Cistercians 7, 32, 37, 39, 58, 61, 64, 74, 76, 88, 91, 100, 183
Citeaux Abbey 50, 58
Clairmont, Council of 17, 32, 183
Clairvaux 91
Clement V 135, 138
Clericis Laicos 130
Cloth Hall, Ypres 33
Cluny, France 18
  Abbey 19
Columbus, Christopher 101, 162
Conrad III of Germany 120
Constantinople 14, 17, 120, 183, 186
Copper Scroll, The 48–9
Cresson, Battle of 120
crucifixion 15
Cyprus 43, 77, 98–9, 128

d'Abbeville, Bernard 188
Dafoe, St.ephen 155, 189
Damascus 118
David I of Scotland 88, 111
de Barverà, Conca 38
de Beaujeu, Guillaume 126
de Blanchefort, Bertrand 159
de Bouillon, Godfrey 26, 38, 43
de Charney, Geoffroy 141, 177–8
de Châtillon, Reynald 123

de Gonneville, Geoffroy 177
de Got, Bertrand 131, 135
de Gumbach, Hugo 140
de Lusignan, Guy 121
de Molay, Jacques 77, 99, 135–6, 141, 144, 150, 176–8, 185
de Molesme, Robert 54
de Montbard, Aleth 60
de Montbard, André 45, 60, 87
de Montdidier, Payen 45
de Montfort, Simon 158
de Nogaret, Guillaume 131
de Payen, Hugues 27, 43, 45, 48, 60, 70, 77, 89–90, 185
de Pérraud, Hugo 177
de Ridefort, Gerard 120, 123
de Saint-Homer, Gaudefroy 27
de St. Amand, Ode 119
de St. Clair, Catherine 89
de St. Clair, William 166
de St. Omer, Geoffroi 45
de St. Omer, Godfrey 64
de St. Omer, Hughes 45
de St.-Amand, Achambaud 45
de Tonnerre, Saint Michel 187
de Tremelay, Bernard 118
de Tyr, Guillaume 42, 44
Dead Sea Scrolls 47, 49, 155, 184
Dijon 59
Dome of the Rock, Jerusalem 37, 65
Dominicans 70
Domme 104
Dordogne 104
Dorylaeum 120
Duc de Berry, Jean 37
Durer, Albrecht 154

Edessa 26

190

Edinburgh 89, 166
Edward I 127
Edward II 138
Egypt 20, 23, 119
Élancourt 143
England 84–5, 99
Eugene II 59

Fabritius, Carel 152
Famagusta 128
Ferdinand II of León 10
Fernández, Alejo 162
First Crusade 17, 23, 34,
    43, 119
First World War 33
Flanders 30, 33, 35, 37
Fleury, J. Robert 26
Formis, Abbey of St.
    Angelo 78, 112
Fouquet 139
Frale, Barbara 176
France 30, 85, 99
Frankish Gauls 30
Frederick I, Holy Roman
    Emperor 113, 125, 186
Freemasonry 155, 166,
    168, 184
Freemasons' Hall,
    London 170
Fulk I 68

Galilee, Sea of 121, 124
Gascony 85, 186
Gondemare 45
Gothic architecture 63,
    109, 184
Grand Lodge of
    England 170
Grand Master 27, 60, 70,
    77, 118, 150, 184
Great Goddess 155
Guillaume X of
    Aquitaine 60
Guy of Auvergne 177
Guy of Lusignan 121

Halifax, England 152–3
Harding, St.ephen 58, 187
Hattin, Battle of 121
    Horns of 121

Hebrew 184
Hebrew Bible 46
Hejaz 21
Henry I of England 87
Henry I of Navarre 129
Henry II 91
Henry the Navigator 101
Herod Antipas 152
Herodias 154
Hierarchical St.atutes 90
High Holborn, London 87
Hiram Key 168, 170
Hochadel, Burgundy 60
holy fire 15
Holy Grail 168
Holy Land 17, 23, 24, 42,
    64, 85, 99, 104, 117,
    134, 143, 155, 184
Holy Sepulcher,
    Cambridge 87, 108
Holy Sepulcher,
    Jerusalem 15, 32, 37,
    185

Île de la Cité, Paris 18
Innocent II 59
Islam 6, 14, 155, 185
Istanbul, Turkey 183
Italy 35

Jacquand, Claude 136
Jaffa 64, 124
Jerusalem 6, 15, 24, 44,
    102, 106, 168
    conquering of 25
Jesus Christ 15, 113, 136
Joan of Navarre 129
John of England 103
John I of Portugal 101
Jordan, River 47, 49
Judaism 9, 25

Kalaun, Sultan 126
Kelso Abbey 111
Kilmartin, Scotland 161
Kilwinning, Scotland 168
Knight, Christopher 168,
    170, 189
Knights Hospitaller 16, 185
Knights of Christ 101

Knights of St. John of
    Jerusalem 43, 54, 135,
    143
Knights Templar 6, 37
Knights, Frankish 23
Knights, German 23
Konya 25
Kurds 122

L'Anse aux Meadows 163
La Bel 130
La Cavalerie 105
La Couvertoirade 104–5
La Rochelle 98–100, 143,
    149, 162
Lagny, France 35
Laidler, Keith 189
Languedoc 159
Laon, France 82
Larivière, Philippe 119
Larzac Plateau 104
lay brothers 61
Lebanon 126
Leigh, Richard 159, 172,
    189
Leopold I of Austria 164
Leopold III, Duke of
    Austria 165
Lessing, Karl Frederick 180
Lincoln, Henry 159, 172,
    189
Lisbon 101
Little Maplestead, Essex,
    England 87
Livre des Passages d'Outre-
    mer 18
Lomas, Robert 168, 170,
    189
London 102
Lord of Tiberius 45
Lord's Prayer 93
Lorraine 38
Lothair, Emperor 60
Louis IX 76
Louis VI of France 60
Louis VII of France 120
Louis XVI of France 151

Magna Carta 103, 185
Mainz, Germany 140

Markale, Jean 190
Mary of Bethany (Mary
    Magdalene) 94
Master of Normandy 141
Mecca 20–1
Medina 20
Mediterranean 7, 20, 34,
    99, 101
Melisende 68
Midi-Pyrénées 105
Molesme Abbey 58
Monmouth 84
Montagne de Reims 34
Montbard 59
Montgisard 98, 116
    Battle of 119
Montier-la-Celle 57
Montségur 159
    Cross of 156
    Battle of 164
Moses 46
Mosque of the Prophet 20
Mount Zion 46
mounted knights 22
Muhammad 20, 155
Muhammad's Tomb 20
Muret, Battle of 158
Muslims 25, 122

Naples 139
Nazareth 120
Nebuchadnezzar 46
Nebuchadnezzar II 188
Netherlands 30
Neufmoustier 186
Newfoundland 163
Newport Tower, Rhode
    Island 163
Nicaea 120
Nicholson, Helen 190
Normandy 30, 177, 186
Notre Dame Cathedral,
    Paris 141
Nova Scotia 99, 101

Oak Island 99
Ognissanti 163
Order of the Temple 7
Orkney, Earl of 162, 166
Oxford University 48

Pais, Gauldim 163
Papal Bull 138
Paris 83, 86, 128–9, 142
Partner, Peter 190
Patzak Hymnal 95
Perestrello, Bartolomeo 101
Persian Empire 20
Peter the Hermit 24, 186
Philip II of France 186
Philip III 129
Philip IV 6, 8, 76, 103, 125, 127, 129, 134, 136, 138, 142, 144, 150, 176, 179
Picknett, Lynn 190
Piece Hall Gate 153
Pignatelli, Bernardo (Eugene III) 59
Plantagenet Kings 112
Poitou 177
Ponferrada, León 10
Poor Knights of Christ 6, 16, 64, 75, 140, 149, 172
Pope Alexander III 39, 44
Pope Benedict XVI 179
Pope Boniface VIII 130–1
Pope Clement V 131, 135, 150, 172, 178–9
Pope Eugene III 91
Pope Gregory III 186
Pope Honorius II 62, 68, 184
Pope Innocent III 130, 156, 159
Pope Nicholas V 176
Pope Pius VII 39
Pope Urban II 16, 17, 23, 32
Portugal 101, 140, 149
Préaux, Abbey of Saint-Pierre 76
Prince of Galilee 45
Prince, Clive 190
Processus Contra Templarios 178
Provins 35–6
purgatory 78
Puy de Dome, France 143

Ralls, Karen 190
Ramleh 119
Raymond of Toulousse 158
Read, Paul Piers 190
Revelation, Book of 26
Richard I of Capua 78, 112
Richard I of England 117, 122, 124, 128, 186
Rievaulx Abbey 91
Robert the Bruce 160, 166
Robert the Burgundian 86
Roche Guillaume, Antioch 104
Roger of Sicily 60
Roman Catholic Church 32, 56, 156, 160
Rome 32
Rosal 45
Rosicrucianism 9
Roslin Glen 166
Rosslyn Chapel 166–8
Round Church, The 87
Rule of Conduct 74

Safed 124
Saffuriya, Springs of 122
Sainte Chapelle 18
Saladin 116, 119, 121–2, 187
Salah-ad-Din-Yusef ibn Ayyub 187
Salome 154
Santes Creus 38
Saracens 17, 32, 148
Saudi Arabia 20
Schonfield, Hugh 155
Schwyz 164
Scotland 83, 84, 89, 91, 99, 161
Second Crusade 118
Seljuk Turks 21, 25
Selkirk Abbey 88
Sempach 164
    Battle of 165
Sens, France 138
Seward, Desmond 190
Sidon 124
Sinclair, Andrew 190

Sinclair, Henry 173
Sinclair, William 173
Solomon's Temple 46
Spain 21, 139, 149
St. Benedict of Nursia 56, 188
St. Bernard of Clairvaux (see Bernard of Clairvaux)
St. Clair, Henry 162
St. Clair, William 166
St. Gregory the Great 76
St. James 10
St. John the Baptist 95, 152, 153
St. Mary Magdalene 94
St. Matthew 166
St. Michel-de-Tonnerre 57
St. Nicholas 102
St. Robert of Molesme 50, 57
St. Sepulcher, Northampton 87
St.auffacher, Werner 164
Sultan Omar 42
Switzerland 74, 164
Syria 23

Templars 9, 16, 71, 83
Templar Church of St. Michael 84
Templar monks 74
Templar navy 98
Temple Church, Bristol 162
Temple Mount 8, 44, 48, 187
Temple of Solomon 6, 16, 27, 64, 75, 140, 149, 168, 172, 187
Tescelin, Lord of Fountaines 59
Theobald II 51
Theobald III 63
Theobald VI of Blois 104
Third Crusade 125
Tiberius 122
Tiron des Chevaliers 104
Tironensians 39, 88, 98, 104, 111, 188

Tissot, James Jacques Joseph 47
Tomar, Portugal 163
Toron 124
Tours, France 176
Trani 163
Tripoli 126
Troyes, France 9, 34, 60, 86, 128
    Cathedral of St. Peter and St. Paul 63, 74
    Council of 43, 63, 78, 87, 116, 184
Turks 43
Tyre 42

Unterwalden 164
Upton-Ward, Judi 190

Vallbona de les Monges 38
Vatican 17, 172
    Library 188
Venice 77
Victoria, Queen 166
Vienna, Council of 140
Vimbodi i Poblet 38
Virgin Mary 94, 155

Wales 84
warrior monks 16, 71
White Monks 91
William I, Duke of Aquitaine 19
William of Tyre 45
    Historia 123

Yahweh 46
Yvelines, France 143

Zacharias 95